Issues in the

Information
Age

Other books in the Contemporary Issues series:

The Environment
Biomedical Ethics
Sports

CONTEMPORARY ISSUES

Issues in the
Information
Age

by Harry Henderson

Lucent Books, San Diego, CA

Library of Congress Cataloging-in-Publication Data

Henderson, Harry, 1951–
   Issues in the information age / by Harry Henderson
     p. cm.—(Contemporary issues)
   Includes bibliographical references (p.   ) and index.
   Summary: Explores the controversies surrounding the impact of
information technology on society such as possible censorship of the
Internet, privacy concerns, and education issues.
   ISBN 1-56006-365-3 (lib. bdg. : alk. paper)
   1. Information technology—Social aspects—United States—
Juvenile literature. 2. Information society—United States—Juvenile
literature. [1. Information technology.] I. Title. II. Series:
Contemporary issues (San Diego, Calif.)
T58.5.H48 1999
303.48'33—dc21   98-36765
                                        CIP
                                        AC

Special acknowledgment to Lori Shein for helping shape the book through her detailed and very helpful suggestions.

Issues in the
Information Age

TABLE OF CONTENTS

Foreword ■

When men are brought face to face with their opponents, forced to listen and learn and mend their ideas, they cease to be children and savages and begin to live like civilized men. Then only is freedom a reality, when men may voice their opinions because they must examine their opinions.

Walter Lippmann, American editor and writer

CONTROVERSY FOSTERS DEBATE. The very mention of a controversial issue prompts listeners to choose sides and offer opinion. But seeing beyond one's opinions is often difficult. As Walter Lippmann implies, true reasoning comes from the ability to appreciate and understand a multiplicity of viewpoints. This ability to assess the range of opinions is not innate; it is learned by the careful study of an issue. Those who wish to reason well, as Lippmann attests, must be willing to examine their own opinions even as they weigh the positive and negative qualities of the opinions of others.

The *Contemporary Issues* series explores controversial topics through the lens of opinion. The series addresses some of today's most debated issues and, drawing on the diversity of opinions, presents a narrative that reflects the controversy surrounding those issues. All of the quoted testimonies are taken from primary sources and represent both prominent and lesser-known persons who have argued these topics. For example, the title on biomedical ethics contains the views of physicians commenting on both sides of the physician-assisted suicide issue: Some wage a moral argument that assisted suicide allows patients to die with dignity, while others assert that assisted suicide violates the Hippocratic oath. Yet the book also includes the opinions of those who see the issue in a more personal way. The relative of a person who died by assisted suicide feels the loss of a loved one and makes a plaintive cry against it, while companions of another assisted suicide victim attest that their friend no longer wanted to endure the agony of a slow death. The profusion of quotes illustrates the range of thoughts and emotions that impinge on any debate. Displaying the range of perspectives, the series is designed to show how personal belief—whether informed by statistical evidence, religious conviction, or public opinion—shapes and complicates arguments.

Each title in the *Contemporary Issues* series discusses multiple controversies within a single field of debate. The title on environmental issues, for example, contains one chapter that asks whether the Endangered Species Act should be repealed, while another asks if Americans can afford the economic and social costs of environmentalism. Narrowing the focus of debate to a specific question, each chapter sharpens the competing perspectives and investigates the philosophies and personal convictions that inform these viewpoints.

Students researching contemporary issues will find this format particularly useful in uncovering the central controversies of topics by placing them in a moral, economic, or political context that allows the students to easily see the points of disagreement. Because of this structure, the series provides an excellent launching point for further research. By clearly defining major points of contention, the series also aids readers in critically examining the structure and source of debates. While providing a resource on which to model persuasive essays, the quoted opinions also permit students to investigate the credibility and usefulness of the evidence presented.

For students contending with current issues, the ability to assess the credibility, usefulness, and persuasiveness of the testimony as well as the factual evidence given by the quoted experts is critical not only in judging the merits of these arguments but in analyzing the students' own beliefs. By plumbing the logic of another person's opinions, readers will be better able to assess their own thinking. And this, in turn, can promote the type of introspection that leads to a conviction based on reason. Though *Contemporary Issues* offers the opportunity to shape one's own opinions in light of competing or concordant philosophies, above all, it shows readers that well-reasoned, well-intentioned arguments can be countered by opposing opinions of equal worth.

Critically examining one's own opinions as well as the opinions of others is what Walter Lippmann believes makes an individual "civilized." Developing the skill early can only aid a reader's understanding of both moral conviction and political action. For students, a facility for reasoning is indispensable. Comprehending the foundations of opinions leads the student to the heart of controversy— to a recognition of what is at stake when holding a certain viewpoint. But the goal is not detached analysis; the issues are often far too immediate for that. The *Contemporary Issues* series induces the reader not only to see the shape of a current controversy, but to engage it, to respond to it, and ultimately to find one's place within it.

Introduction

Opportunities and Challenges

COMPUTERS, DATABASES, NETWORKS, the Internet, the World Wide Web—they seem to be everywhere today. According to government estimates, the number of people using the Internet in the United States and Canada is doubling every one hundred days. Most of today's students will be working tomorrow in jobs where using information technology is essential to success. As the National Academy of Sciences points out, the way Americans work has radically changed in only a generation:

> People graduating from high school or college will average six to eight jobs over the course of a career, many of them requiring skills unforeseen today. About half of all employed Americans work with information—analyzing information that already exists, generating new information, storing and retrieving information.[1]

This trend is likely to accelerate as the twenty-first century begins. Forecaster William E. Halal predicts that

> a "knowledge economy" will likely develop in the United States during the decade of 2000–2010 as automation reduces the need for blue-collar [industrial] and service workers. [About] 60%–70% or so of the workforce may then be composed of knowledge workers: skilled manufacturing teams, information system designers, managers, professionals, educators, scientists, and the like.[2]

13

Learning to benefit from all that information technology offers while avoiding its pitfalls represents the challenge of the twenty-first century.

The new information technology, linked together with the Internet and displayed in homes, schools, and workplaces, offers many promises: richer educational experiences, greater business productivity, more convenient shopping, and exciting new forms of recreation and social interaction. But each application of the technology also raises troubling questions and challenges people to find ways to maximize benefits while reducing risks.

A Wave of Social Change

The information technology revolution is challenging every institution in our society. The capabilities of on-line communications and the Internet are changing the ways students learn, businesses operate, consumers make purchases, and even how people socialize.

In schools, for example, computers and on-line resources offer a new and powerful tool for teaching most skills and academic subjects. How best to use this tool is still a matter of debate. To rely too heavily on a new and unproven technology may work against the best interests of students who, regardless of all the excitement over the new technology, still need a well-rounded education to succeed.

To ignore this new technology, on the other hand, or to waste it on outdated ideas about teaching is to assure that students will be unprepared for their futures.

The information age has also challenged society's notions of free speech and the protections that guarantee it. In the past, the ability to communicate to a wide audience was reserved to those who could afford printing presses—or at least to those writers who could get published. With the Internet, however, anyone can make his or her ideas available to a worldwide audience. Of course, some of the material on the Internet is likely to offend some people because of sexual, political, or other content. The reaction to the free-wheeling Internet and its diverse content has been a vigorous debate that has pitted the constitutional right of free expression against the desire to keep inappropriate material away from kids. Free speech advocates, antipornography crusaders, Internet experts, and librarians each bring their agenda and their priorities to the debate over what should be the "rules of the road" for the information superhighway.

To what degree should today's schoolchildren take advantage of the new technology? A balance between old and new ways must be found.

Ideas about privacy must also be reconsidered because of the widespread use of information technology in every aspect of government, business, and health care. Marketers, hospitals, insurance companies, employers, and government agencies collect a mind-boggling amount of data about every person, starting with the hospital bracelet that identifies a newborn baby all the way to the paperwork for grandpa's funeral. Many people become alarmed when they learn that the organizations that collect all this information are usually not required to reveal that they are doing so, and they don't have to ask permission to distribute or even sell the data to others.

Marc Rotenberg, director of the Electronic Privacy Information Center, suggests that "Privacy is to the information economy what environmental protection was to the industrial economy. This new economy is incredibly productive and important, but there are costs. We are now confronting these costs."[3] Businesses, labor unions, consumer groups, privacy advocates, and legislators are debating a variety of proposals to regulate the collection and distribution of personal information in both the marketplace and the workplace.

A Place Called Cyberspace

Increasingly, the on-line world is not just this provider or that service: It is one great, sprawling *place*, big and as bustling and exciting as Los Angeles or New York. The on-line world, sometimes called the "information superhighway" and sometimes "cyberspace," has many different aspects, as Internet writer Nicholas Trio notes,

> Your business may exist in cyberspace. Your social life may be conducted in cyberspace. You may attend classes in cyberspace. Businesses build cybercafés, cybernewsstands, and cyber front offices. . . . Strangers meet in cyberspace. People feel comfortable enough to reveal themselves in cyberspace. You can disguise yourself in cyberspace. As acceptance of cyberspace as a place grows, so do the demands on the behavior of the inhabitants. The rules governing behavior in cyberspace provide evidence that the Internet has become a society.[4]

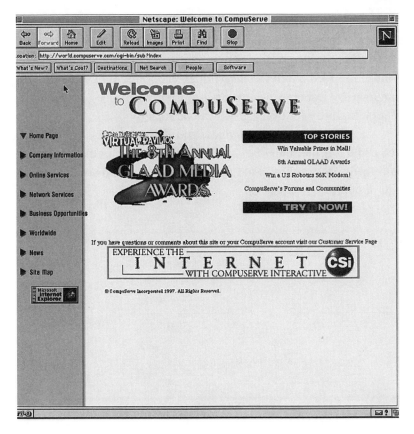

A gateway to cyberspace, which offers countless ways for people to gather information, interact socially, and explore new horizons.

The Internet has increasingly become a social outlet, a place where people meet, share common interests, and develop a sense of community. But as people develop "virtual communities" based on their recreational and cultural interests, it is not clear whether they will still be able to share common values. Neighbors who use the Internet to surf the world may not find the time to talk across the backyard fence. Here, too, people must strike a balance between new possibilities for interaction and people's necessity to deal with their "real world" surroundings and the physical environment.

Finally, although the exciting information revolution has already delivered so much and promises so much more, Internet experts and social thinkers alike are concerned that some people may be left behind because of their race, poverty, age, or other factors. People who don't learn the skills and don't make the on-line connection face an increasingly bleak economic future. Politicians and industry leaders are debating how to provide access to the information highway for every group in our society.

The opportunities, challenges, and debates of the information age come together into one theme: How can we gain the benefits of information technology and the Internet while dealing with the risks and possible consequences?

Chapter 1

How Should Computers Be Used in the Classroom?

I N THE FALL OF 1997 the board of education of the nation's second most populous state heard a bold proposal from its chairman Jack Christie: Dump all the old textbooks and, instead of buying $1.8 billion worth of new ones, get every one of the state's more than 3 million students a laptop computer with a CD-ROM drive and access to the Internet. A student in Christie's proposed all-electronic schools could simply pop a CD-ROM into the computer and access the latest information on world events. For even more up-to-date information, that student could plug the computer into a phone line and dial into the Internet, clicking on websites that are specially designed to provide reference material and help with homework.

The uproar over Christie's idea was immediate. Critics worried aloud about not only the cost of buying millions of laptops but the need to constantly maintain and upgrade them to keep up with advances in software. They also warned that the computers, which would probably cost about $1,200 apiece, would provide enterprising thieves with a potential gold mine.

The other big concern, expressed by teachers and administrators around the state, had to do with quality of education. These educators worried that years of carefully designed courses of study supported by textbooks and other materials would be abandoned, leaving the state's young people without the necessary elements of a well-rounded education.

The debate over replacing textbooks with computers in Texas represents a discussion that is now under way in school districts nationwide. That issue is not so much about whether to use computers in education, for nearly all today agree that young people must master computer skills to succeed in the modern world. Rather, the issue is one of defining how computers and the many on-line resources should be used in the classroom.

In education, as in so many other areas of modern life, people are being challenged to find ways to get the benefits of rapidly evolving technology while avoiding possible traps. This is a difficult task, for as Spud Van de Water, an educator who chaired a meeting to discuss Christie's proposal, points out:

> People have a very strong sense that they've got to figure out how to make technology a positive force in education, but they don't have those answers themselves. . . . Part of the problem is that the pace of research [in educational use of computers] is not as quick as the pace of new technology and the applications of that technology.[5]

While replacing textbooks with laptop computers may seem like a good idea, equipment costs, hardware and software obsolescence, and theft must be considered.

Growth of Computing in the Schools

If there was ever any doubt about the importance of preparing the nation's young people for life in the information age, it has long since faded. Politicians (both Democrat and Republican) as well as educators have proclaimed that Americans must prepare for the twenty-first century by connecting everyone to the information superhighway—the Internet and World Wide Web with its torrent of information, resources, and services.

Business leaders and education experts have agreed that computer literacy—knowing how computers work and how to use them—is essential for the success of future generations. The emphasis on computer skills seems to be justified. During the 1980s and 1990s, the fastest economic growth in America has been in the "high tech" area, including the computer hardware and software industries that sprung up in places such as "Silicon Valley," south of San Francisco. Most of the classified job ads in newspapers now require skills such as word processing, spreadsheets, database operations, or programming. A person entering the workforce without computer skills will find opportunities to be increasingly limited.

Starting in the 1980s, schools began to buy microcomputers such as Apple IIs (and later, Macintoshes and IBM compatibles) with the aim of teaching basic computer skills to all students. By the mid-1990s, most educators realized that the basic skills of how to operate a computer would not be enough. The introduction of the Internet expanded the definition of computer literacy to include the mastery of on-line communications and information retrieval.

A nationwide campaign called NetDay has brought thousands of volunteers into American elementary and high schools to wire them into the worldwide network. President Clinton has described NetDay as "an inspiration to the nation . . . a modern version of an old-fashioned barn raising." It was important, he said, because "We are putting the future at the fingertips of your children and we are doing it in the best American tradition."[6]

The penetration of the Internet into schools is starting to become evident. A *USA Today* poll in April 1997 revealed that 56 percent of American students have used the Internet in some way for a school

*An avid supporter of wiring classrooms into the worldwide network,
President Bill Clinton has described these efforts as "putting the future
at the fingertips" of the nation's elementary and high school students.*

project, and 77 percent of students say they prefer using the Internet
to using books and magazines.

How Computers Are Being Used in the Classroom

In some schools and school districts, computer learning mainly consists
of classes in such skills as word processing, computer graphics, and
programming. Computers are placed together in a computer lab, and
groups of students take turns using them. Meanwhile, the traditional
classes such as social studies, reading, and composition taught during
the rest of the day have little or no involvement with computers.

In other schools and districts, computer learning is joined with the teaching of many subjects. In this way the personal computer (and especially the ever-expanding Internet) becomes a general-purpose tool that makes it possible for students to explore and learn any subject in ways that may not be possible with just pencil, paper, and printed books.

Many examples of the merging of computers and traditional teaching tools can be found in schools today. Many textbooks, encyclopedias, and other reference materials, for example, are now available on CD-ROM. The equivalent of a $1,500, thirty-volume printed encyclopedia can fit on one or two CDs costing less than a tenth of the price. Such electronic encyclopedias offer yearly updates and even the ability for readers to link directly from an entry to websites that provide expanded information and up-to-date developments. Efforts such as the Gutenberg Project and the Library of Congress American Memory Project are creating electronic archives that include the text of hundreds of classic books as well as original historical sources (such as letters and public documents). A class studying life on a pre–Civil War Southern plantation, for example, can now work with many of the same materials that professional historians use in their research.

In addition to providing reference materials, computer software can also help students master facts and skills. Since the 1970s, computer-aided instruction (CAI) software has also been in widespread use. In CAI, the computer generates a series of carefully arranged questions or exercises on a subject such as math, spelling, or geography. The software can also present a quiz and automatically grade the students' answers. (Simpler, more colorful versions of CAI are also marketed for preschool and elementary school students in programs, such as *Math Blaster* and *Reader Rabbit*, that offer gamelike activities that can help familiarize beginners with arithmetic facts, word parts, sentence construction, and reading.) Advocates of CAI point out that the software can serve as an always patient instructor that offers students instant feedback and that can tailor the difficulty of the questions to the students' skill levels. Students can learn at their own pace, and the built-in testing can keep teachers informed about their progress.

CAI does have the drawback of being rather rigid with its question-and-answer format. But many computer game simulations—even those not marketed as educational software—offer rich, interactive worlds that players can use to explore such subjects as history, ecology, and economics. For example, while children can learn geography facts from a CAI program, they can also play games such as *Civilization,* and learn how to balance research, economic resources, military forces, and settlements to create a functioning empire. They can play *Sim City* and take on the role of a mayor who must respond to the people's demand for housing, transportation, and jobs. Games such as *Sim Life* can be used to teach scientific concepts such as evolution and genetics, or the interaction of predator and prey species.

Learning with the Internet

Most CAI and simulation programs are "stand-alone" activities with one student (or perhaps a small group) at the computer answering questions or manipulating objects on the screen. But as the Internet has become part of the classroom, students are increasingly becoming involved in projects that use on-line communication and research.

The Internet does offer many of the features of stand-alone software—reference databases, news services, programs to help teach particular subjects, simulations, and games. But for many users, the most exciting thing about the Internet is the ability to communicate directly with other users around the world, by posting messages in newsgroups or electronic bulletin boards or by typing messages back and forth to other users in chat rooms.

The Global SchoolNet Foundation promotes the use of the Internet in schools and provides many resources for teachers and students. Its website points out many of the advantages of the Internet as a source of educational activities. For example, a student reading about pollution in a traditional textbook can absorb information only passively. However, a group of students can use the Internet to connect directly to instruments that are measuring various forms of pollution in their area. They can help gather actual data to help scientists in their research. They can create reports that high-

The Global SchoolNet Foundation website offers many Internet-related resources for teachers and students.

light environmental problems and design a web page that provides links to groups that are trying to do something about them.

Such Internet projects do more than just teach students about a particular subject. As the Global SchoolNet Foundation points out on its website,

> Web projects build learning experiences on the kind of learning one does throughout life, rather than only on "school" subjects. By using the real tools for intellectual work that are used in the workplace, rather than oversimplified textbook techniques, students become familiar with the kinds of knowledge that exist. Finding information and people on the Internet gives students the knowledge of how to go about acquiring the knowledge they may need.[7]

Cooperative projects, involving students from varied backgrounds—in their own communities and in other communities or even other countries—are one of the most intriguing features of the Internet. The Global SchoolNet Foundation has posted dozens of web pages featuring such cooperative educational projects. For example, "Stamp on Black History" creates a mosaic of African Americans who have been honored on postage stamps for their contributions to the country and relates their achievements to the movements of American history. "Collab-O'Write" lets students write and post their own short stories or rewrite existing stories by changing their outcome. Successful Web-based projects can carry on from year to year as each class adds its own contribution. Teachers and students anywhere in the world can join in a project or use it as an inspiration and a source of ideas for creating their own efforts.

Sometimes, however, the most important learning comes from the personal contacts students make across geographic or cultural barriers. In 1989, for example, Jeff Golub and his fellow high school students in Seattle joined with students abroad to research global pollution through the Internet. One day a fellow student in Berlin sent a message not about pollution but about how young German people were gathering with tense eagerness around the wall that had divided the western and eastern portions of the city for nearly thirty

Young Germans gather atop the Berlin Wall prior to its dismantling in November 1989. Students from around the world learned of and took part in this historic event through contacts made on the Internet.

years. The Germans were wondering whether the wall might soon come down, restoring Berlin as part of a united Germany. After two weeks of messages, it finally did.

Two years later, Golub's class was connected to something called the Learning Network. Again, they were studying pollution. In January 1991, one of the participants, a girl in Tel Aviv, Israel, started her message by noting that Scud missiles had landed and described her neighborhood as it faced Iraqi missile attacks during the Persian Gulf War. Each day the Seattle students checked their e-mail to see if their correspondents were OK. One Seattle student asked them when they were most afraid. The teenagers in Tel Aviv replied that they were afraid to take showers, because the missile alert might come in while they were wet, naked, and unable to hear. They might not make it to the sealed room that each family had prepared in their house to protect them against a possible poison gas attack.

Many advocates believe that this ability to engage students in the real world is the most exciting thing about wiring schools to the Internet and making it a key part of the education process. In a global economy where an event in the Middle East may affect markets in Tokyo and New York in a matter of minutes, the Internet is becoming a vital link for business, government, and ordinary citizens trying to cope with rapid worldwide change. Students who become used to communicating and gathering information internationally will be best prepared to function in the global economy.

A Matter of Priorities

Although it is easy to paint an exciting picture of how computers and the Internet may be the centerpiece of the twenty-first century classroom, many critics have raised both practical and philosophical objections to any headlong rush to replace traditional and proven teaching tools with a technology that is evolving and still largely unproven. They also worry that money diverted to computers, software, and training will rob other urgently needed educational programs, services, training, and equipment.

The running of a school involves many competing goals and priorities. Public dissatisfaction with the performance of many schools has led to state boards of education requiring that particular skills such as reading or arithmetic be emphasized in the curriculum, or course of study that students are expected to complete. Requirements for programs such as special education and bilingual education must also be met. At the same time, schools have been forced to address serious social problems of poverty, violence, and drug abuse. Programs addressing this variety of concerns compete for the money the school receives from taxes and government grants each year. Although schools can sometimes get government or corporate grants to fund special projects, computers must generally compete with many other priorities in setting school budgets.

Even maintaining school buildings—especially aging ones—takes money, and money isn't always available even for that purpose. Viewers of TV news programs in the San Francisco Bay Area in 1997 could see upbeat feature stories about NetDay volunteers bringing the information superhighway to Oakland's inner-city schools. But other reports about those same schools showed leaking ceilings, broken windows, missing locks, and filthy bathrooms. Clifford Stoll, an astronomer turned computer expert, has written a book called *Silicon Snake Oil* that suggests that the Internet has been overhyped as a solution to the challenges of maintaining a high-quality public education system. He points out that

> Our schools face serious problems, including overcrowded classrooms, teacher incompetence, and lack of security. Local education budgets barely cover salaries, books, and paper. Computers address none of these problems. They're expensive, quickly become obsolete, and drain scarce capital budgets.[8]

As a practical matter, a major investment in computers usually means that something else must be sacrificed. The Kittridge Street Elementary School in Los Angeles, for example, canceled its music program to pay for hiring a person to manage its computer programs. In the Mansfield, Massachusetts, school district, a proposal to hire art, music, and physical education teachers was dropped in favor of spending $333,000 on computers. Critics point out that art, music, and physical education all involve activities that are vital to

the development of well-rounded individuals, and they are activities that require a "live" teacher interacting with students, not just a pre-programmed machine.

The Challenge for Teachers

Schools or districts that decide to make a major commitment to the use of computers and on-line resources cannot simply connect their computers and begin teaching. Teachers must help students learn to use them and guide their learning activities. But many teachers learned their profession before desktop computers and the Internet had come on the scene. They may be less familiar with computers than many of their students. Often there is little provision for training teachers in computer use. According to educator Damon Moore, "We're at an F in training. Most teachers have very little knowledge as to what's available online. They know about the Internet, but they've never seen or used it." [9]

Resources for teaching teachers about the Internet and how to use it in the classroom are becoming available, however. In Montana, for example, teachers in tiny one- and two-room schools had been isolated from each other and from the resources that could help them plan their classes and use technology effectively. In 1988, Frank Odasz, a former rancher with a degree in educational technology, founded the Big Sky Network. It used a simple computer bulletin board to link twelve libraries and forty schools. Using this network, teachers began answering each other's computer questions, sharing lesson plans and projects, and evaluating educational software.

The Computer as Tool

Growing use of educational software and the Internet raises the question of what role computers should play in the classroom, and what effect this will have on the job of the teacher. The simplest possibility is that computers will be just another tool in the classroom, like pen, paper, or calculators. Even in that role, they may be a quite useful tool. For example, sixth grade teacher Monica Daw noted that her students used to take a whole week to complete a particular writing assignment. But when the class got laptops with word processing programs, students began to turn in their work days ahead of schedule. Further, Daw says that the quality of the writing has also improved because it is much easier for students to revise and polish their work: "With a computer they can highlight, erase it and do it over. It might sound silly for us, but it's a big deal to them. Rewriting the whole thing is like the end of the world for them." [10]

One attraction of the "just another tool" approach to computers is that little change in the curriculum or the organization of the school is needed. Many schools simply set up a computer lab and give students an hour or two a week to learn word processing, spreadsheets, databases, or charting programs. The students are then free to use the software in doing their reports or projects for their other classes.

Teacher's Assistant?

Going beyond the computer lab to the everyday classroom, teachers can use CAI software as a substitute for traditional workbooks and photocopied sheets of exercises to provide practice in skills such as spelling or multiplication. By freeing the teacher from having to create worksheets or grade quizzes, computers may give him or her more time to work with students individually.

Some critics such as Massachusetts Institute of Technology computer education expert Seymour Papert complain that CAI soft-

A school computer lab offers students a chance to acquire needed skills but may not be the most creative form of learning.

ware is too often used as a *substitute* for creative teaching, amounting to "little more than 'a thousand-dollar flash card' and they disparage what it does as 'drill and kill.'"[11] And while the programs often dress up the lessons with animated graphics and musical "rewards" for correct answers, many students quickly become bored with them. Nevertheless, developmental education expert James Kulik, after examining five hundred different studies, concluded that students in classes that used CAI software learned more and learned faster than their counterparts in traditional classes.

To keep students' interest (and to impress their parents), educational software developers try to make their educational software more graphic- and action-oriented, more like a video game. But Marilyn Durch, a high school English teacher, believes that glitzy software may contribute to students' short attention spans: "Computers are lollipops that rot your teeth. The kids love them. But once they get hooked, they get bored without all the whoopee stuff. It makes reading a book seem tedious. Books don't have sound effects and their brains have to do all the work."[12]

Other critics point out that, while it may be easy to use CAI, it is not the most creative use of the technology, and it may only hide the shortcomings of the school. Alan Kay, whose pioneering work helped develop the multimedia industry, described his misgivings in 1995:

> Perhaps the saddest occasion for me is to be taken to a computerized classroom and be shown children joyfully using computers. They are happy, the teachers and administrators are happy, and their parents are happy. Yet, in most such classrooms, on closer examination I can see that the children are doing nothing interesting or growth-inducing at all! This is technology as a kind of junk food—people love it but there is no nutrition to speak of. At its worst, it's a kind of "cargo cult" in which it is thought that the mere presence of computers will somehow bring learning back to the classroom.[13]

Computers can also be used to improve communications between teachers, students, and parents. Some classrooms are wired

as local networks with e-mail and bulletin board features. Instead of writing a homework assignment on the blackboard, the teacher can simply e-mail it to the students. After students go home and start working on the assignment, they can (if their family has a home PC) e-mail their questions to the teacher and get answers even during the evening or on the weekend.

The positive side of this kind of classroom communication is that it may free teachers from the often crushing burden of routine paperwork and give them more time to work with students. But in colleges, where e-mail has been in use for a longer time, Clifford Stoll fears that "the computer is a barrier to close teaching relationships. When students receive assignments through e-mail and send in homework over the network, they miss out on chances to discuss things with their prof. They don't visit her office and catch the latest news. They're learning at arm's length." [14]

Creative Learning

The computer can be used in wonderfully creative ways. Seymour Papert, activist and inventor of LOGO (a programming language designed especially for beginners), has spent decades studying how computers might be used to unlock a more joyful, creative approach to learning. As an example, he describes a student named Henry who had become quite a computer whiz, specializing in computer graphics. However, Henry complained that the screen displays he programmed, while technically very adept, were not very exciting or graceful.

One day he saw Brian, a fellow student, dancing in the school corridor. Intrigued by his ability to improvise sequences of dance movements, Henry suggested to Brian that they team up to write a new program that would create "screen choreography" (dance steps) using animated computer graphics. After many hours of work, they succeeded.

Papert points out that in the course of the project, Henry and Brian had to master mathematics that were more advanced than called for in the curriculum. But, he insists, "beyond developing technical mathematical skills, they came to experience mathematics in a very different way. It became something to be used purposefully;

they felt it as a source of power in pursuing important and deeply personal projects." [15]

Henry and Brian used the computer not to help them absorb prepackaged knowledge but to create a computer graphics project that would capture some of the spirit of dance. To succeed, they had to master mathematical tools and use them creatively. They also had to work together as a team, bringing together Henry's mathematical and programming skills and Brian's understanding of visualization and movement.

Henry and Brian's collaboration came about pretty much by accident. But this type of learning experience could be folded into the school semester on a regular basis. Many students would undoubtedly benefit from such projects. But critics worry that students who are struggling in such basic areas as reading and simple math might be left behind.

The field of education has had a decades-long debate over what focus teaching should take. This debate is between those who believe education should stress fundamentals—basics such as English grammar, reading, and multiplication facts—and those who advocate an emphasis on teaching thinking skills. In public schools, it has seemed that one approach must dominate because there isn't enough time in the school day to satisfy both.

The computer may offer a way to redefine the terms of the debate. Effective CAI software might help students master the basics in less time—and some of the time saved might be used for more creative, open-ended projects like Henry and Brian's computer dancing. Further, if the "one size fits all" approach of traditional textbooks and teaching plans could be replaced by CAI and individualized instruction, students who are struggling to catch up to grade level could receive extra help without holding back their more advanced classmates.

The teacher, of course, plays a key role in any educational method. The two general approaches to education imply different roles for the teacher. In the traditional approach, the teacher is the source of facts, or at least the guide who organizes the students' efforts to master facts. With the Internet, however, education might become more like a series of projects that is controlled more by the

In traditional instruction, a teacher is the primary source of facts and the guide in students' efforts to master those facts.

students than by the teacher. In this approach, as suggested in a report by the National Academy of Sciences, teachers become

> guides or mentors who help students navigate through the information made available by technology and interactive communications. They help students gather and organize information, judge its value, and decide how to present it to others. Moving from group to group and from student to student, teachers help students stay focused and working at the limits of their abilities. When the class meets as a whole, teachers share the responsibility for teaching with the students—each of whom has been forging ahead at his or her own pace.[16]

The Internet takes education beyond the limits of the classroom. Students can work on projects throughout the day, even after school

*In a less traditional form of instruction, a teacher helps a student
navigate through the many turns of the information superhighway.*

or on weekends. The classroom is no longer the center of the educational process but a place where teachers and students meet for face-to-face communication. Already many colleges are offering classes where students view lectures and carry on class discussions via the Internet, with little or no physical contact. It is possible this "distance learning" may someday extend to high schools or even elementary schools.

The Future of the Classroom

There is no sign that the drive to bring computers into classrooms and to wire schools to the Internet is slowing down. The concerns of parents and industry leaders about preparing students for the twenty-first century information society remain strong. At the same time, the competing interests of traditionalists and innovators make it unlikely that either approach will win out completely.

It is difficult to measure the effect of computers on education. Perhaps because there are so many different ways to use computers in schools, it has been difficult to draw clear comparisons between computerized and traditional teaching methods. In September 1998, however, the Educational Testing Service released the first conclusive large-scale study of the effectiveness of computers in the classroom. Surprisingly, it found that students who spent more time using school computers actually did worse in math tests than students who used the machines less. The detailed findings, however, suggest that the problem is not with the computers but with how they are used. Eighth graders who used computers for drill and practice exercises scored more than half a grade lower than students who used computers in other ways. On the other hand, students who used the computers for simulations that helped them visualize math concepts scored higher by two-fifths of a grade level. The overall poor results are caused by the fact that computers are still used much more often for drill than for simulation.

Although educators are still struggling to find the most effective ways to use them, it is clear that computers in education are here to stay, and they will play an increasingly important role in the classroom. But it is less clear how much they may eventually change how teachers teach and students learn.

Chapter 2

Should the Internet Be Censored?

L IBRARIANS AT THE SAN JOSE, California, public library thought they'd hit on a good idea for expanding service when they set up fifty-eight computers that would give library users access to the Internet. In doing this, librarians felt they were carrying out the primary duty of their profession—making the whole range of on-line information and images available to everyone, including those too poor to afford home computers. Based on surveys of library patrons, the librarians expected public interest in the new service to be high, but they did not expect to be embroiled in a controversy over pornography, or sexually explicit images and writings.

Shortly after the Internet computers had been installed at the library, several members of the Reverend Randy Wing's church congregation complained to him that children were gathering around library terminals, giggling and snickering as they viewed and downloaded pornographic images. People started to complain to the city council. San Jose, like many communities, was caught up in the issue of whether to censor the Internet in order to protect children from harmful materials or exploitation.

An increasing number of city and county library boards have recently forced libraries to install software on their public Internet terminals that automatically blocks access to material that is too sexually explicit or that is otherwise considered objectionable. The American Library Association opposes this trend, because librarians have historically defended the right of all library users to free access to all materials. It does not want librarians to be put in the role of being censors of either books or the Internet.

After parents complained about children viewing pornography at the San Jose library, council member Pat Dando proposed that the city require that blocking software be installed in every library Internet computer that would be used by children. (Children could use unrestricted adult terminals with parental permission.) Dando argued that "It's the city's responsibility to ensure that when parents drop their children off at a San Jose public library, they feel reasonably assured that the kids are spending healthy productive time and not watching sex acts on the Net." Mayor Susan Hammer objected, however: "I can't think of anything worse than government and politicians getting into the role of acting as censors."[17] The city council turned down Dando's proposal by an eight-to-three vote.

The San Jose library controversy illustrates how new technology such as the Internet promises many benefits but also challenges users to find a way to minimize potential harmful effects. The Internet makes available a tremendous variety of web pages that offer everything from health care tips to sports news to help with school projects in science, social studies, and the arts. But a more disturbing side of the Internet was revealed when a growing number of websites began to offer pornography, sexually explicit "chat" communications, and

other materials that might be appropriate only for adults—but were often freely available to children.

The Cyberporn Controversy

Most Americans first heard about the existence of pornography on the Internet from the July 3, 1995, issue of *Time* magazine. The cover showed the face of a child bathed in the eerie glow of a computer screen. The blurb read: "Cyberporn . . . EXCLUSIVE: a new study shows how pervasive [widespread] and wild it really is. Can we protect our kids—and free speech?" The article described how researchers at Carnegie-Mellon University had discovered that the Internet was filled with explicit graphics showing just about every possible form of sexual activity, including depictions involving children.

Experienced Internet users such as "cyberlaw" expert Mike Godwin were concerned that the *Time* article would provoke a public outcry that would lead to pressure to censor or regulate the Internet. At his suggestion, Vanderbilt University marketing professor Donna Hoffman began to analyze the Carnegie-Mellon study, which had been carried out by an undergraduate researcher named Marty Rimm. She found what she (and many other Internet experts) considered to be a fundamental flaw. The on-line world includes many separate dial-up bulletin boards that are not connected to the Internet. Many of these feature adult material, but they require a paid "subscription" before they can be accessed. Focusing on these stand-alone boards (and some Internet newsgroups) gave the impression that the entire Internet was saturated with pornography. In fact, the vast majority of websites had nothing to do with sex at all. But in 1995 Internet users were still a rather small minority of Americans, and many people (including politicians) who would become involved in the cyberporn controversy had little knowledge of how the Internet actually organizes and distributes material.

Many experienced Internet users hoped that as people learned more about the Internet the controversy would subside. But while Rimm had considerably overstated the case in 1995, there definitely was a growing amount of pornography on-line. By 1997 there were about seventy thousand sex-related websites, making up a considerable chunk of the $4 billion a year adult-entertainment industry.

Many of these sites require payment by credit card for access, making it unlikely that children would be exposed to them. But there are also chat lines on more family-oriented on-line services such as America Online where users can indulge in interactive fantasies or "cybersex." Writer Dinty Moore describes a typical session:

> Two people sit alone in front of their respective computers, anywhere in the world. They type onto the screen a description of what they might be doing to one another if they were not separated by three thousand miles, marriage, total lack of acquaintance, and the fact one of them is really just a thirteen year old boy pretending to be a voluptuous blonde woman of twenty five.[18]

Many parents don't want *their* thirteen-year-old boy (or girl) indulging in such conversation. And some worry that such encounters will go beyond mere conversation. Alarming stories have appeared in the media about how adults are engaging children in on-line chats and then persuading them to meet them personally so they can molest them or persuade them to pose for pornographic pictures. "I call the Internet the playground of the nineties for pedophiles,"[19] says Donna Rice Hughes, a director at Enough Is Enough, an antipornography group. Cases of Internet contacts leading to molestation are rare, with only twenty-three cases involving chat rooms reported between 1994 and 1996 by the National Center for Missing and Exploited Children. But the possibility of "cyberpredators" exploiting children on-line helped fuel the demand that the government do something to protect children from pornography and sex chat.

Whether on-line or in print, pornography involving children is illegal. But groups such as the American Civil Liberties Union (ACLU) and the newly formed Electronic Frontier Foundation worry that public alarm about on-line pornography and exploitation of children could lead to laws that would ban other on-line material that courts have declared to be permissible for adults, including explicit discussion about sex. Advocates of such laws say that they are just trying to protect children. But as technology writer Denise Caruso points out, "The argument 'we're doing this for your own good' is a slippery slope when applied to free speech."[20]

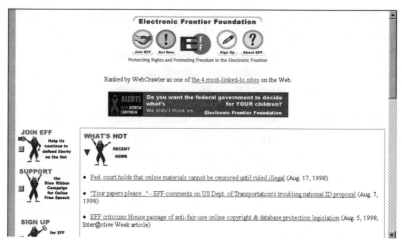

The website of the Electronic Frontier Foundation, which objects to curbing pornography on the Internet if that infringes on the reading and viewing preferences of adults.

If sexual material is banned because it might be harmful for children, the same argument can be used to ban material that is violent or hateful or that offends some particular group of people. People and groups differ about what is offensive and what is acceptable. Conservative and Christian fundamentalist groups tend to focus on sex, while some liberal groups are more concerned about the portrayal of violence or the use of racial slurs. For civil libertarians (advocates of individual rights), the key issue is whether the freedom of speech guaranteed by the First Amendment to the Constitution would apply to the websites, newsgroups, and chat services of the Internet. If not, and if every group gets to censor whatever it finds objectionable, the information superhighway might soon narrow down to a one-lane country road.

The Communications Decency Act and Its Critics

Congress acted quickly to respond to the public's concerns. At the time of the cyberporn article, Congress was debating a law dealing with the telecommunications industry. Included in the legislation was an amendment called the Communications Decency Act, or CDA. The CDA declared the transmission of "obscene, indecent, or patently offensive"[21] pornography over the Internet to be a crime.

With no major public hearing and little debate, the amended legislation was passed by Congress on February 1, 1996. One week later, it was signed into law by President Clinton.

The ACLU immediately filed suit in federal court to block the law. Civil libertarians had two main objections to the CDA. The first had to do with the language referring to "indecent" material. In 1973 the Supreme Court made a distinction between "obscene" material and "indecent" material in the *Miller v. California* case. The justices said that whether material was obscene would be determined by asking questions like the following:

1. Is it designed to be sexually arousing?
2. Is it arousing in a way that one's local community would consider healthy or immoral?
3. Does it show acts whose depictions are specifically prohibited by state law?
4. Does the work, when taken as a whole, lack significant literary, artistic, scientific, or social value?[22]

Under those standards, pornography depicting children is almost always considered obscene, and thus illegal. But there is also a whole range of material that might be considered "indecent,"

Used with the permission of Ed Gamble.

though not obscene, and also be illegal. The courts have said that community standards must be considered in determining whether material is indecent or "patently offensive." This ruling recognizes the fact that a cosmopolitan area such as New York or Los Angeles is likely to be more tolerant of sexual material than, for example, a small rural town in Georgia.

The problem is that the Internet connects communities into a single, seamless communications web. A person who sets up a website in California may post material that is not indecent by California standards. But Georgia has stricter standards. What happens when someone in Georgia accesses the California website? Which state's standards would be used to determine whether the material was legal?

Indeed, the Internet is worldwide, and on-line service providers such as CompuServe have users in many nations. In 1995 officials in Mannheim, Germany, deemed certain materials on CompuServe offensive. CompuServe decided that it had to remove the material because it had no way to determine whether someone was logging on from Germany.

Critics of the CDA were worried that the same thing would happen throughout the Internet. The CDA prohibited making indecent materials available to children under eighteen. Critics argued that the new law would force service providers that wanted to avoid criminal charges to restrict the whole Internet to material suitable for children since they couldn't determine the age of their users. This was comparable to all theaters having to show only G-rated movies because young people can sneak through the doors.

The authors of the legislation said that on-line service providers could avoid censorship by restricting their website or chat area to adults. They would have to check the age of anyone who tried to enter. Critics pointed out that the only way to check ages on-line was by requiring credit card numbers, which could be verified by their issuers. Since people under eighteen years of age generally don't have credit cards, young people could be kept out of adult areas. But credit cards can only be used by commercial sites, where people pay for access. The many sites run by individuals and non-profit groups would have no way to check age and thus be forced to censor their material.

The Supreme Court Decision

The ACLU suit argued that the CDA would subject Internet users to far greater restrictions than exist in other media such as printed books or magazines. This, they said, violated the right of free speech guaranteed by the First Amendment.

A panel of federal judges took a crash course on the Internet to familiarize themselves with the kinds of material people were worried about. After listening to the arguments about free speech and the impracticality of enforcing the new law, they issued an injunction, or order that the law be set aside. Federal District Judge Stewart Dalzell declared that the Internet was not really different from the speech or printed books that the First Amendment was intended to protect. The new technology was just the latest way people could express themselves:

> The Internet may fairly be regarded as a never-ending, worldwide conversation. As the most participatory form of mass speech yet developed, the Internet deserves the highest protection from government intrusion. . . .

> Just as the strength of the Internet is chaos, so the strength of our liberty depends upon the chaos and cacophony [loud noise] of the unfettered speech the First Amendment protects. For these reasons, I without hesitation hold that the CDA is unconstitutional on its face.[23]

Supporters of the CDA argue that the Internet is more like broadcasting than like a newspaper and therefore should be subject to the same rules that forbid certain obscene language and sexual activity in broadcast programs. But the judges disagreed. Children at home can turn on a TV or radio and be immediately confronted by offensive material. Courts have held that this justifies holding all broadcast channels and programs to some minimum standards of decency. With the Internet, however, the user has to ask for material specifically, by clicking on links or choosing to subscribe to services. Since material does not come without being requested, the Internet is more like a magazine or newspaper than like TV. Courts have always given magazines, newspapers, and other printed material

DRAWINGBOARD / DANZIGER

Step 1. Make sure server contact to network modem process may be if option menu netscape preferences or applications for link toolbars if images browse mail fetch ircle ircle FreePPP or PPPop and reload or disable config Eudora dialup icon serial port thing stuff hello hello ring-no-answer yadda yadda poohbear...

JEFF DANZIGER, Christian Science Monitor

Jeff Danziger. © 1995 Los Angeles Times Syndicate.

Supreme Court will rule on Internet decency, but uh ... first they have to ... um ... connect to the Internet.

ial wide freedom of speech under the First Amendment. Essentially, the judges had put the Internet in the same category.

The government appealed the judges' decision, but on June 26, 1996, the Supreme Court voted unanimously that the CDA violated the First Amendment guarantee of freedom of speech and would have threatened to wipe out a large portion of the Internet community by making it hard, if not impossible, to discuss adult matters on the Internet.

Self-Regulation

The Supreme Court's ruling means that the government cannot prevent Internet sites from carrying material that is not legally obscene. However, it might be possible to label web pages to indicate that they are not suitable for children. Parents might be able to use the labels to decide whether their children would be allowed to view the material.

This idea is not new. Movies are rated G, PG, R, and so on to indicate whether they are suitable for young children, teenagers, or adults only. Rating systems are also starting to be used for television. People in the Internet industry have begun to talk about a voluntary system where websites would provide similar ratings for their offerings.

Seth Warshavsky, chief executive of Internet Entertainment Group in Seattle, one of the nation's largest sex-related websites, warned his industry that "If we don't self-regulate, then the government eventually will. These [suggestions] are positive moves. The industry can do a much better job than the government. We understand the medium much better."[24]

Even schemes such as those that are similar to movie ratings give cause for worry, however. A rating system might make service providers reluctant to carry material that is suitable only for adults, just as many theaters do not show X-rated films. David Greene, program director for the National Campaign for Freedom of Expression, believes that public pressure for such ratings may make it difficult to devise a system that protects the rights of adults while safeguarding children. "I'd like the industry to ensure that free speech isn't overlooked. But based on everything that's going on, I'm not too sure about that."[25]

Major media companies such as Time and CNN object to having a "one size fits all" Web rating system. If instituted, this system would work like the television v-chip, a proposed device that would be included in all new TVs and could be used together with a system of ratings to control what could be watched.

Vice President Al Gore and others feel that parents, not government, should be responsible for what children see on the Internet.

On the other hand, conservative groups such as the Family Research Council believe that a voluntary rating system does not go far enough. While theaters can turn kids away from X-rated movies, Internet ratings are simply advisory and don't actually block access. Young people who want to view adult material would not be barred from doing so unless a parent or other adult stood watch at the computer. Also, if the rating system is purely voluntary, some sites may ignore it entirely.

Software Solutions

In an effort to restrict access to material considered inappropriate for young people, without infringing on the rights of adults, software makers have come up with one possible solution: software that identifies objectionable material and automatically blocks access to it. Programs such as *CyberPatrol*, *SurfWatch*, and *NetNanny* are now available as part of what is on its way to becoming a flourishing industry. Many industry leaders see the blocking software as a way parents can keep control of their children's use of the Internet without compromising free speech for adults.

Unfortunately, as a report from the Electronic Privacy Information Center (EPIC) notes, filtering programs also block young people from obtaining much useful information that has nothing to do with pornography. This is because many filtering programs use lists of keywords such as *sex* or *breast*. When the user attempts to access a website, the program compares the site's description to the keyword list. If a forbidden keyword is found, the site is blocked and the user sees only a message that says that access is denied.

It turns out that many sites that aren't involved with pornography have the forbidden keywords somewhere on their pages. EPIC made a list of such sites, including ones for the American Red Cross, the Bill of Rights, and the Smithsonian Institution. Even the poetry of Anne Sexton can be blocked because of the "sex" in her last name. Since they don't consider the context in which words are used, filter programs are likely to block a site that deals with safe sex education once it finds the word *sex,* or refuse to show a site devoted to breast cancer research because it finds *breast*.

Some blocking software takes a different approach. Instead of scanning for keywords, the software manufacturer maintains a list of acceptable Web addresses. The program allows only acceptable sites to be accessed. Critics point out two problems with this approach. First, the user must accept the manufacturer's judgment about what material is acceptable. Second, manufacturers can evaluate only a tiny fraction of the hundreds of thousands of new web pages created every month. An attempt to create a "kid-safe zone" out of a tiny corner of the Internet would be likely to cut off much of the Internet's most useful resources.

The response to the blocking software solution has not all been favorable. Groups such as the Family Research Council believe that blocking software does not address the real problem of the spread of pornography in our society, and it sticks parents with the responsibility for monitoring an industry that should be regulated by government. Cathleen A. Cleaver, director of legal studies at the Family Research Council, believes that relying on the software

Educators and software developers are searching for ways to restrict children's access to inappropriate material in cyberspace, short of those which were once used to ban textbooks.

is bad philosophically because it advocates restricting the behavior of the "good guys" (families and children) while giving license to the "bad guys" to litter cyberspace with pornography. It also represents a drastic departure from time-honored principles of the role of law in protecting children from exploitation. Outside cyberspace, laws restrain people from displaying sexually explicit images in public places and from selling alcohol, tobacco, or porn magazines to children.[26]

Advocates of free speech also have problems with the use of blocking software. While it has no problem with parents using it at home, the American Library Association opposes installing the software on the public access Internet computers in libraries. It does not believe that libraries should be in the business of deciding what material is appropriate for users to read. The ACLU also opposes the use of blocking software in libraries. As an alternative, it suggests that students undergo training before they are turned loose to travel the information superhighway:

> Successful completion of a seminar similar to a driver's education course could be required of minors who seek Internet privileges in the classroom or library. Such seminars could emphasize the dangers of disclosing personally identifiable information such as one's address, communicating with strangers about personal or intimate matters, or relying on inaccurate resources on the Net.[27]

In other words, children should learn to use the Internet safely just as they will eventually learn to drive safely.

Empowering the Individual

All of the proposed solutions to the Internet pornography problem, ranging from censorship to ratings to blocking software, have their shortcomings (and their critics). In the end, the responsibility usually falls on parents. Parents are often told that they need to take an active interest in what their children are doing on-line. As Sergeant Nick Battaglia, former supervisor of the child exploitation unit of

the San Jose Police Department, points out, "Just like you wouldn't let your child play alone in an urban park for three hours, you shouldn't let them play alone on the Internet."[28] But in many families it is the children, not the parents, who are computer savvy. Many parents may work in traditional jobs that don't use computers much, if at all, while the children are growing up with a computer mouse in their hand. Parents' lack of experience makes it hard for them to supervise their children or to help them find appropriate material.

The safety versus free speech debate will continue. Every proposed solution involves a tradeoff. Censorship offers the most protection for children but cannot be implemented without restricting the freedom of adults. Rating systems might protect children but require more cooperation from industry and more effort from parents than is likely to be achieved. Blocking software, a technological "quick fix" for a technological issue, would preserve adults' rights but make the Internet much less useful as a learning tool for children. Different families (and communities) are likely to strike different balances between freedom and safety.

Chapter 3

Does Privacy Need Greater Protection?

WHEN MARI FRANK got the call demanding immediate payment, she laughed. It must be some kind of silly mistake. She certainly hadn't bought $11,000 worth of merchandise from a local toy store. Nor had she bought a new Mustang convertible or any of the $50,000 worth of merchandise that had been charged in her name.

A thief had contacted an information broker—someone skilled at searching on-line databases and providing information for a fee. Pretending to be a licensed private investigator, she bought a copy of Frank's credit file from the broker. With that file, she had everything she needed to apply for a credit card in Frank's name—Social Security number, bank account numbers, and Frank's record of good credit. The thief had stolen Frank's identity and gone on a shopping spree. Frank's own credit was now ruined. While she didn't have to pay the bills, she would have to deal with endless phone calls and paperwork and wait many months to clean up her credit record.

Frank was a victim of "identity fraud," a fast-growing crime that thrives on the huge databases of personal information that are compiled daily by credit bureaus, banks, and stores. The Secret Service reported 8,686 arrests for this offense in 1996, and 9,455 arrests in 1997. But that is just the tip of the iceberg. Many fraudulent credit card charges go unnoticed and unreported. Many that are reported have insufficient evidence for prosecution or even investigation. But credit agencies get tens of thousands of calls every year from credit card customers who believe they are being defrauded.

Fraud has always existed, of course, carried out using paper-work such as bogus checks, forged signatures, and fake IDs. The ability to defraud was limited, however, by the difficulty of getting information about the individual to be impersonated. The information usually had to be physically stolen, such as by snatching a purse or copying a number from a credit card slip in a restaurant. But the combination of on-line databases and the Internet has made fraud much easier for skilled thieves. The Internet makes it easy to search databases and easy to compile data from people's web pages, purchases they make on-line, or information they might volunteer in a contest, survey, or loan application.

Automatic teller machine databases were once vulnerable to thieves who used the stored information to withdraw funds from customer accounts.

A New Vulnerability

The average computer user might have a hard time gathering all of this personal information, but anyone who is skilled in searching the Web could probably locate at least some of it. With a few key pieces of information, the treasure trove of personal data can be unlocked. The author of a manual for on-line investigation claims that

> In a few hours, sitting at my computer, beginning with no more than your name and address, I can find out what you do for a living, the names and ages of your spouse and children, what kind of car you drive, the value of your house, and how much you pay in taxes on it. From what I learn about your job, your house, and the demographics of your neighborhood, I can make a good guess at your income. I can uncover that forgotten drug bust in college. In fact, if you are well-known or your name is sufficiently unusual, I can do all this without even knowing your address.[29]

In addition to credit fraud, personal information can be used to uncover assets for a divorce or lawsuit, by employers who want to pry into the lives of their employees, or by the media pursuing a celebrity. The gathering of personal information can have legitimate uses, such as in law enforcement, but there are few controls over data searches by private individuals.

The routine storage of vast amounts of information on computers and the ability to conduct all kinds of transactions on-line (ranging from credit card purchases to automatic bill paying and banking) have brought convenience but also vulnerability. Phone numbers, addresses, Social Security numbers, bank account numbers, credit information, and even medical records, and workplace correspondence are more open to prying eyes than ever before, thanks to on-line databases and the easy-to-use Internet.

Back in 1977 the federal U.S. Privacy Protection Study Commission warned that "The real danger is the gradual erosion of individual liberties through the automation, integration, and interconnection of many small, separate record-keeping systems, each of which alone may seem innocuous [harmless], even benevolent, and wholly justifiable."[30]

Today that interconnected web of information has emerged in the form of the Internet.

Public concern about misuse of private information shows up in polls, such as a 1997 telephone survey conducted by *Money* magazine. According to the results, 74 percent of the public are somewhat or very concerned about threats to their privacy, and 29 percent have experienced at least one serious invasion of their own personal privacy. About two-thirds of the respondents said they are more worried about their privacy now than they were five years ago.

Privacy, which has been described by commentator Alan F. Westin as "the claim of individuals, groups, or institutions to determine for themselves when, how, and to what extent information about themselves is communicated to others,"[31] has become less certain, and people have become correspondingly more anxious about it. Today many people fear they have lost control over how the information they provide in the course of daily life will be used. It is in this atmosphere that society seeks to balance the convenience and efficiency of information technology against the risks of theft, fraud, and loss of privacy.

Collecting Consumer Information

In 1994 U.S. companies held more than 5 billion data records, including 400 million credit files. The collection and distribution of this information is a major industry. Much of this information processing is necessary if people are to enjoy the convenience of credit cards. If a store is going to let someone walk out the door with a $5,000 big-screen TV, it needs to know that the consumer has good credit, and the credit bureaus can only verify credit by keeping track of each person's purchases and of whether they have paid their bills on time.

However, the store would also like to know what other products might interest the TV purchaser, and it would like to find the names of other people to whom it could target its advertising. Since the store (or its advertising agency) is willing to pay for this valuable information, the information from credit applications or product registration cards becomes the raw material for creating mailing lists and databases for marketers. Indeed, with the widespread use of checkout

Supermarket checkout scanners gather detailed facts about consumer purchases, product preferences, and spending habits.

scanners in supermarkets and other stores, it is easy to gather detailed information about a customer's most routine purchases.

Since the mid-1990s, consumers seem to be flocking to the Internet, where they can view detailed information about products and then order them with a few mouse clicks. By the end of 1997 about 10 million Americans and Canadians had bought something over the Internet. On-line bookstores such as amazon.com and Barnes and Noble have become big businesses.

To process orders, websites must collect names, addresses, and credit card information. In the early days of the Internet, such information was sometimes sent in a form that could be easily read by people who broke into computer systems. Today, however, most transactions are carried out by "secure server" software that automatically encrypts the information—puts it into a code that cannot be read without the proper key. This makes it less likely that people's credit card numbers will be stolen while they travel over the Net, although an unscrupulous employee (or a fake website) could still steal and decode the information.

Order processing is not the only area of vulnerability. Many companies ask their customers to fill out on-line forms that ask for information such as their age, income, and whether they have bought or are planning to buy various products such as audio or computer equipment. Additionally, websites often download small data files called cookies to users' computers, usually without asking first. The cookies can be useful because they can store information (such as the user's address and preferences) to save time on later visits to the site, but the information is often collected without informing the consumer or getting permission. (Users can set their Web browsing software to reject cookies, however, or to ask whether a given cookie should be accepted.) While cookies usually don't do real harm, they feel like an invasion of privacy to many people.

Consumer Information Abuses

The value of consumer information often drives companies to gather it without much regard for the consequences to consumers. As one writer on privacy issues notes: "Laws on privacy may vary from country to country, but the laws of economics do not. The laws of economics in the information age say that information has value—it is a product that can be sold, just like socks, cars, and toothpaste." [32]

The industry spawned by the developments in information storage, collection, and retrieval grew so quickly that it soon outstripped the traditional methods of government regulation or oversight. Many people were surprised—and dismayed—when they learned how their personal information was being used—or abused.

For example, the Lexis-Nexis database company admitted that it paid credit bureaus for Social Security numbers and credit information on millions of Americans. In June 1996, it sold the information to direct marketers and distributed it over the Internet. Lexis-Nexis was sued in a consumer class action and forced to remove Social Security numbers, and it agreed to remove anyone's name from its database on request.

Privacy watchdog groups began to stir public concern about the unregulated distribution of consumer data, and that concern began to be heard. In 1991, software developer Lotus Development Corporation and Equifax, a major credit bureau, announced plans to sell *Households*, a CD-ROM database containing names, addresses, and marketing information on 120 million consumers. But after thirty thousand people wrote or called demanding that their names be removed, the companies abandoned their plans.

By July 1998, the Federal Trade Commission (FTC) had begun to crack down on businesses that collect information from Internet users without telling them what they are collecting or what they will do with it. For example, the commission got an agreement from GeoCities Corporation (a web page provider) that it would disclose its information-gathering practices to its 2 million customers and allow users to delete information from its database.

A Demand for Regulation

Consumer privacy advocates don't think correcting abuses on a case-by-case basis through lawsuits or settlements is enough, however. They believe more comprehensive regulation is needed. Almost 1,000 of the 7,945 bills introduced in the 104th U.S. Congress dealt with privacy issues in some way. These included a bill by Senators Dianne Feinstein (Democrat from California) and Charles Grassley (Iowa Republican) that would prohibit credit bureaus from selling personal identifiers such as mothers' maiden names, birthdates, unlisted phone numbers, and Social Security numbers.

Vice President Al Gore has proposed an "electronic bill of rights" for the digital age that would give consumers control over how information they provide on-line will be used. He stated that

> Americans should have the right to choose whether their personal information is disclosed. They should have the right to know how, when and how much of that information is being used. And they should have the right to see it themselves, to know if it is accurate.[33]

While Congress debates privacy bills, many business groups, such as the Business Software Alliance and the Consumer Electronics Manufacturers Association, have responded to the growing demand for regulation of information use by developing standards

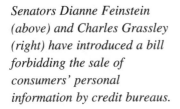

Senators Dianne Feinstein (above) and Charles Grassley (right) have introduced a bill forbidding the sale of consumers' personal information by credit bureaus.

that businesses would agree to follow voluntarily. Under such a system a business would agree to have an independent agency monitor its information gathering. In return, the business could display a "seal" on its web page that would assure consumers that it followed approved practices, such as disclosing the kinds of information it gathers and whether it distributes the information to other businesses.

While this type of response from business has won some praise, it may not be enough where young people are concerned. Marketing to children has become big business: According to the Center for Media Education (a watchdog group that monitors TV advertising targeted at kids), young people spend $80 billion each year, and they influence another $160 billion of spending by their parents. Many companies are designing websites especially for kids. Shelley Pasnik, director for children's policy at the center, describes such websites as "a powerful digital data collection machine, designed to extract enormous amounts of personal information from children on a routine basis."[34] The Nickelodeon channel's website, for example, offers a chance to win prizes in exchange for names and addresses. While Nickelodeon says it does not sell this information to anyone, a March 1998 FTC survey revealed that only about 15 percent of websites (including those aimed at children) had an on-line notice that described what they would do with the information they collected.

Advocates for regulating on-line information-gathering point out the lack of control over who can obtain information and the possible hazards of allowing this new industry to operate without regulation. For example, a TV reporter ordered fifty-five hundred names of children from a marketing company called Metromail using the name of Richard Allen Davis, convicted murderer of twelve-year-old Polly Klaas of Petaluma, California. If the reporter had actually been a child molester, the information could have been used to try to locate, meet, or even kidnap the children. To prevent such abuses, proposals in Congress and by the FTC would require that a parent give permission before information could be collected from children under twelve-years-old.

A Healthy Concern

The heart of the privacy issue seems whether people have the right to decide how information about their identity or activities will be used. Abuses generally involve failing to ask for permission before collecting or using the data. The need for control over personal information is perhaps greatest where a person's health is concerned.

Traditionally, medical records were kept confidential between a patient and his or her doctor. Indeed, the ancient Hippocratic Oath taken by many doctors pledges that "Whatsoever things I see or hear concerning the life of men, in my attendance on the sick or even apart therefrom, which ought not be noised abroad, I will keep silence thereon, counting such things to be as sacred secrets."[35]

Today, however, doctors often must share a patient's medical records with insurance companies and health maintenance organizations (HMOs) for whom they work. Growing pressure to control high medical costs has led some insurers to cancel coverage when they receive certain information about patients. For example, if an insurer or employer finds out someone has a serious (and expensive) medical condition such as AIDS or cancer, that information might lead to a person losing insurance or perhaps not being hired. A survey by University of Illinois professor David Linowes in 1997 found that 35 percent of employers use information such as that derived from medical insurance claims or requests for leave to help make hiring, firing, or promotion decisions. Of course, medical information must be gathered for many legitimate reasons such as to prevent fraudulent insurance claims, to determine where to build hospitals, to track the spread of infectious disease, and to be able to warn patients who may be taking a dangerous combination of prescription drugs.

There's no guarantee that something as simple as a trip to the pharmacy won't result in information being disclosed to third parties. In 1992, a nationwide drugstore chain gave the Southeastern Pennsylvania Transportation Authority (SEPTA) a list of employees

Medical information can in some cases be disclosed to third parties without a patient's knowledge or consent.

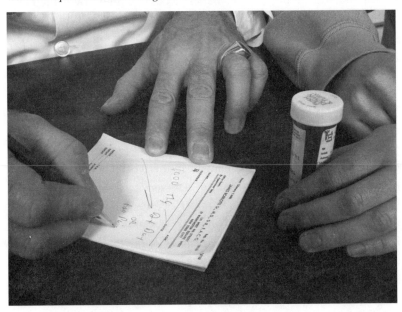

who had bought more than $100 worth of drugs a month. A supervisor at SEPTA used this information to find workers who were using Retrovir, a drug used to treat AIDS. Although a court eventually ruled that SEPTA had not caused much actual harm, the potential for abuse is clear.

Individuals concerned about the misuse of their medical records probably would not find much relief if they turned to the government for help because of the lack of comprehensive national regulations. According to Donna E. Shalala, secretary of health and human services, "Our private health information [is] being shared, collected, analyzed, and stored with fewer federal standards than video store records."[36]

A 1993 report from the federal Office of Technology Assessment says that the existing "patchwork" of state and federal laws is not adequate for protecting consumers. Information systems gather and combine data from many states, making it very hard to determine which state's law might apply in a given situation or which information provider might be held legally responsible for abuses.

By mid-1998, however, the Clinton administration and members of Congress were proposing regulations that would give people much more control over who gets to see their medical records. Proposals include giving people better access to their own medical records and the ability to correct false information they find, as well as prohibiting insurance companies from discriminating against people whose family medical history or genetic information suggests that they may develop a serious illness.

Privacy in the Workplace

As legislators and judges try to carve out standards for protecting medical information, they face an equally complicated issue when it comes to the information exchanged in the workplace. Most workplaces today use computers and on-line services, particularly electronic mail, which has become almost as essential as the telephone for business communications. Computer systems provide invaluable help with processing and storing information that is vital to the smooth functioning of any business. They also offer employers new ways to monitor the activities and efficiency of their workers.

Many managers monitor workers' phone conversations. If someone

Secretary of Health and Human Services Donna E. Shalala has noted the absence of safeguards protecting medical records from disclosure or misuse.

is working at a computer or automated phone system, software can record the worker's typing speed, error rate, and how long it takes to handle a phone call.

This type of monitoring can inspire workers to work harder, but it can also lead to stress. William Wresch recounts the comment of one worker in a mill where

> [the computer] sees every move [workers] make while on the job, yet they cannot see the computer's "eyes" buried deep in the back of their computer, recording every piece of information that floats by, sending it off to a report that only the office manager sees. . . . Says one mill employee, "With this information on the computer, there has been a psychological effect. We know there is something that will tell on us exactly. We can't fudge it now, so we hustle more."[37]

Besides watching what workers are doing, employers can also monitor what they are saying on the phone or in electronic mail. Several cases in which an employee thought an employer's surveillance went too far have found their way into the courts. For example, in March 1989, Alana Shoars began to work as e-mail administrator for Epson America, Inc., a large electronics manufacturer. As part of her job, she instructed employees in the proper use of e-mail, including the use of passwords and other safeguards to protect messages from prying eyes.

About six months later, however, she discovered that Robert Hillseth, her supervisor, had been regularly intercepting and printing out all the e-mail sent or received at Epson's offices in Torrance, California. When she confronted him with her discovery, he fired her. She then sued Epson, claiming (among other things) an invasion of the privacy of Epson workers.

Shoars argued that the workers had an "expectation of privacy"—that is, that since they had to use a password to access the e-mail system, they could assume other people would not be able to read their messages. Epson, on the other hand, argued that the e-mail system was just another business tool, provided to help employers do their jobs more efficiently. As a business tool, it was under the control of the company, it said, and employees had no right to expect they could use it to send personal messages that would be kept private. In July 1992 the court agreed with the company's argument and threw out Shoars's class action suit.

Employers argue that they must watch the workplace to prevent losses or to detect behavior such as sexual harassment that can easily lead to costly lawsuits. They worry about employees selling valuable business secrets to competitors. The growing use of the Internet has also led employers to monitor workers' Internet use to discourage use of the Net for entertainment or other personal purposes. Monitoring workers and eavesdropping on e-mail may be legal in most cases, but it can harm businesses. The feeling of living in a fishbowl may lead workers to have low morale, and thus lower productivity.

To some extent, striking the balance between monitoring and acknowledging privacy will be determined by a compromise between employers and employees in each workplace. In some cases, labor unions raise privacy issues and win concessions from between employers and employees in each workplace. In some cases, labor unions raise privacy issues and win concessions from employers. Other privacy advocates have gone to Congress to seek stronger protections. It is unlikely that all monitoring in the workplace will be banned, but new laws may require that employers tell their workers how and when they are being monitored, and employers may be required to show that their surveillance has a legitimate

Employees who use company e-mail for personal business may find themselves receiving an unwelcome message.

Protecting Privacy with Cryptography

Most people agree that some form of law is needed to ensure that society benefits from information technology while still being protected from invasions of privacy. Passing laws may not be the only way of achieving this goal, however. Software that blocks unauthorized reading of information is already available. Data such as e-mail messages or credit card transactions can be encrypted—turned into coded messages that can be read only with the proper key.

Encryption could reduce identity fraud and other information crimes by making it impossible for hackers to read credit card numbers and for snoops to read private e-mail. Speaking before the Committee to Study National Cryptography Policy of the National Research Council in April 1995, Shari Steele, a lawyer for the Electronic Frontier Foundation (a group of privacy advocates), pointed out:

> In order for the information superhighway to reach its full potential, network security must be assured. Kevin Mitnick [a convicted hacker], who stole users' passwords as they logged on and used those passwords to break into computers across the network, could have been stopped with encryption. If the passwords, credit-card numbers, and long-distance toll access codes he stole had been encrypted, he would not have been able to make use of the information he obtained.[38]

The Clipper Chip: An Acceptable Compromise?

Law enforcement authorities have expressed concerns about encryption software, however. They believe that criminals could use encryption to conceal records relating to illegal gambling, money laundering, and other unlawful activities, or use encrypted e-mail to plan crimes. When police have sufficient cause to believe a crime has been committed, they can get a warrant to seize computer files, but what good is the evidence if the police can't read it because it is encrypted? As security expert Dorothy Denning notes:

> If we fail to pass legislation that will ensure a continued capability for court-ordered surveillance, systems fielded

without an adequate provision for court-ordered intercepts would become sanctuaries for criminality wherein Organized Crime leaders, drug dealers, terrorists, and other criminals could act with impunity [no fear of punishment]. Eventually, we could find ourselves with an increase in major crimes against society, a greatly diminished capacity to fight them, and no timely solution.[39]

Federal officials believed that they had found a way to let people use secure codes while still allowing the government to decode information that might be criminal evidence. They proposed that all new computers manufactured in the United States include a "clipper chip," a special chip that provided encryption services. In order to use the encryption, however, users would have to register with a government agency that would hold their decoding keys "in escrow." If police obtained a court order, they could get the key from the escrow agency and use it to read the information.

There were immediate objections from Internet and civil liberties groups that asked: Who could guarantee that the government would not misuse its access to the decoding keys? As policy analysts Kenneth W. Dam and Herbert S. Lin noted:

Many businesses and individuals do not see the value in using escrowed encryption because dependence on a government-approved product is likely to slow innovation, and they worry about the security of the extra copy of the decryption key.[40]

As a result of the storm of criticism, the clipper chip idea has been largely withdrawn.

Pretty Good Privacy

The clipper chip proposal may also have failed because alternative methods of cryptography have been available for free on the Internet for a number of years. In 1991 a programmer named Phil Zimmermann released a program called *Pretty Good Privacy*, or PGP. This program uses a kind of coding called public-key cryptography. It uses a mathematical formula to generate pairs of keys based on a very large

To what degree should the government have access to personal information in its fight against crime? The "clipper chip" would have allowed police to decode encrypted e-mail messages and computer files.

prime number. The keys in a pair have a special relationship: Text encoded using one of the keys can only be read using the other key.

A person can distribute one key in the pair, called the public key. Anyone using the public key can encode a message that can be read only by the person holding the corresponding private key. The private key itself need never be sent anywhere, so no one can steal it. Further, if one receives a message encoded with a person's private key, one can be sure it was sent by that person. The private key can thus serve as a "digital signature" that verifies the identity of the sender.

Zimmermann at first planned to sell his program to users, but he later decided to distribute it for free. He believed it was important that his program be available to anyone who wanted it, because, he said,

If privacy is outlawed, only outlaws will have privacy. Intelligence agencies have access to good cryptographic technology. So do the big arms and drug traffickers. . . . But ordinary people and grass-roots political organizations mostly have not had access to affordable military-grade public-key cryptographic technology. Until now.[41]

Zimmermann is not alone in his view that the average person has a right to decide which personal information should remain private and which should be revealed, when, and to whom. Eric Hughes, a self-declared "cypherpunk" (cryptography activist), declares that

[Strong] privacy is necessary for an open society in the electronic age. Privacy is not secrecy. A private matter is something that one doesn't want the whole world to know, but a secret matter is something one doesn't want anybody to know. Privacy is the power to selectively reveal one's self to the world. We must defend our own privacy if we expect to have any. We must come together and create systems which allow anonymous transactions to take place.[42]

By the late 1990s, most computer users were not using encryption (except indirectly, through secure credit card transactions). The federal government has made it illegal to use some kinds of hard-to-break codes or to export such coding systems to other countries because of concerns that they might be used by spies to conceal their activities. But it is doubtful that any kind of software can be restricted for long when it can be distributed anonymously via the worldwide Internet.

Striking a Balance

The information age has spawned many competing interests when it comes to privacy. Generally, people want to protect their personal information from being used without their consent, but they are willing to sacrifice some privacy for the convenience of using credit cards or making purchases on-line. They know that one can't run any large health care provider without keeping detailed records, but

THE CENTER FOR DEMOCRACY & TECHNOLOGY PRIVACY QUIZ

PRIVACY ON TRIAL
★ THE LEWINSKY-STARR EDITION ★

Privacy Quiz!

Do you know your privacy rights?

Privacy stories in the news -- Do they have anything to do with
you and your privacy?

Monica Lewinsky's book purchases. Linda Tripp's telephone
tape recordings. Newt Gingrich's cell phone conversations. A
sailor's "profile" on a large internet service provider. Recent
sensational stories in the national media have highlighted the

*Privacy rights, as highlighted by the Center for Democracy &
Technology's website, will remain an important issue of the future.*

they want assurances that the records will not be revealed to a third
party without their consent. People do not want to surrender their
privacy to an employer without being given a good reason. In general, people want to be able to make an informed choice so they can
decide whether a possible benefit to themselves or society is worth
the loss of privacy.

As privacy expert Fred Cate points out, society will have to
decide on a series of compromises in which the costs of privacy are
balanced against its importance and value to the individual:

> Individuals and institutions as a whole share an interest in
> identifying and facilitating those means—including pri-
> vacy—that are necessary to achieve desired ends. What is
> needed is a balance, of which privacy is a part.
>
> An important part of that balance is recognizing that pro-
> tecting privacy imposes real costs. It [makes it easier to
> spread] false and misleading information, increases the cost
> of providing products and services, and interferes with
> meaningful evaluation of students and employees. Privacy
> conflicts with other important values within the society,
> such as society's interest in free expression, preventing and

punishing crime, and the efficient operation of government. Privacy even conflicts with what may seem to be more mundane [ordinary] interests such as the desire for instant credit, better targeted mass mailings, lower insurance rates, [and] faster service when ordering merchandise by telephone.[43]

It is hard to predict how the balance between privacy and convenience in the information age will turn out. It is likely, however, that there will be stronger laws to protect personal information (particularly that relating to finances or health). Cryptography will be used to make personal e-mail and ordering merchandise on-line safer, but privacy advocates and law enforcers will continue their age-old struggle between privacy and crime prevention.

Chapter 4

Is Cyberspace Bringing People Together or Splitting Them Apart?

ICK AND SUSAN Tresch Fienberg were worried that their eight-year-old boy John was spending too much time playing with his video game machine. Perhaps, they thought, there was a way to replace that electronic time-waster with something that educated while it entertained. They decided to take his game machine away and give him a personal computer instead. They were pleased with the variety of educational software they could buy for it, including intellectually stimulating games like *Sim City* and they bought a nice assortment of programs. John also seemed to be happy with the new machine.

When they went by their son's room, however, they noticed that more often than not the screen was not displaying *Sim City* or an educational product but "shoot 'em up" games like *Wolfenstein 3-D*. It turned out that John was getting the games from friends or down-loading them from bulletin boards or the Internet.

The Fienbergs soon realized that replacing the game machine with the PC had not accomplished their goal. John was playing the same kind of games he had before, and he was spending more and more hours at the PC. Rick Fienberg told an interviewer that

> [John] doesn't have a lot of other passions. If we didn't actively go upstairs and yank him off, he'd fall asleep in front of [the computer]. He used to play chess, he used to like music, he used to sing a lot. He seems no longer interested in

72

those things. The computer has displaced the other activities in his life.[44]

Many young people do become very involved with computers, and this has given rise to concerns about them failing to develop social and communications skills. Indeed, the computer "nerd" is a stereotypical loner with no friends or social skills. But like all stereotypes, it does not tell the whole story. The information age also opens up new possibilities for social life.

The ability to link computers together into networks has made it possible to reach out, to communicate, and to create new kinds of social interaction ranging from role-playing games to conferences where people converse for many months on politics, music, science fiction, parenting, or any number of other topics. As users exchange messages with the same people day after day, friendships, feuds, even love affairs blossom. Something very much like a small town can emerge—a community where everyone knows everyone else, and cares about what happens to them.

The growth of on-line "virtual communities" raises important questions. People who share common interests or backgrounds—

hip-hop fans, Vietnam veterans, gay teenagers, or dozens of other groups—can find friendship and support on-line that may not be available in their own neighborhood. It is possible that young people like John may be more socially active than their parents realize, but in a way that's different from the way they interacted when they were young. On the other hand, there is the danger that young people, as well as adults, can become so involved with the world inside the computer that they lose interest in school or work, or in doing things with their family or friends. It seems that the powerful new communications technology of computer networks can bring comfort, closeness, and friendship to some people while further isolating those who have limited skills and opportunities.

The Internet as Social Outlet

The Internet began as a military project for coordinating key computers and communications systems in time of war. As college students and others began to join the growing network, however, the emphasis changed to the idea of connecting people with similar interests. During the 1980s, college students connected to the ARPANET (the Internet's ancestor) began to create elaborate shared worlds called multi-user dungeons, or MUDs. Although their software had only words without pictures, the creators of these worlds could write elaborate descriptions of underground rooms, monsters, magical weapons, and quests to find hidden treasures. To undertake the quest, players who connected to the game had to create characters and then have the characters play roles such as fighter, healer, or magician. The group, or "party," of characters had to learn to cooperate in order to be able to defeat the monsters.

Soon the MUD idea went beyond fighting monsters and exploring for treasure. Psychologist Sherry Turkle describes an elaborate on-line Star Trek game that took on the features of a community, complete with work and family life:

> Thousands of players spend up to eighty hours a week participating in intergalactic exploration and wars. Through typed descriptions and typed commands, they create characters who have casual and romantic sexual encounters,

hold jobs and collect paychecks, attend rituals and celebrations, fall in love and get married.[45]

Turkle and other experts point out that this sort of virtual community might become a substitute for what participants refer to as "RL" (real life). An extensive study by Carnegie-Mellon University released in August 1998 concluded that the more people use the Internet, the more depressed and lonely they are likely to become. Although the people being studied used the Internet socially to communicate with people on-line in e-mail and chat rooms, they tended to spend less time with family members. They also made fewer friends in the surrounding community. Because on-line relationships aren't as satisfying as face-to-face ones, people may end up feeling more lonely and depressed even while interacting with many people on-line. It is like eating junk food that fills you up without providing any real nourishment. While some experts have criticized the study for not directly comparing Internet users with nonusers, the results certainly give cause for concern.

On the other hand, the Internet can provide an opportunity to practice social skills in an environment in which one cannot be physically hurt, or it can enrich the life of someone shut in because of illness or disability. The value of the Internet for information and communication must be balanced against other uses to which the

Rising Computer Use

Hours of use per person per year

Media	1990	1996	2001*
Television	1,470	1,567	1,551
Radio	1,135	1,091	1,072
Home Video	38	49	60
Video Games	12	26	37
On-line Computers	1	16	39

*Projections

Source: Veronis, Suhler & Assoc.

time could be put. The appropriate amount and kind of Internet use will depend on each individual's personality, lifestyle, and needs.

The Growth of Virtual Communities

As users engage in continuing on-line conversations, a number of bulletin boards and conferencing systems have developed a sense of permanent community. One of the oldest is the Whole Earth 'Lectronic Link (WELL) in the San Francisco Bay Area. As WELL pioneer Howard Rheingold described it in 1987,

> There's always another mind there. It's like having the corner bar, complete with old buddies and delightful newcomers and new tools waiting to take home and fresh graffiti and letters, except instead of putting on my coat, shutting down the computer, and walking down to the corner, I just invoke my telecom program and there they are. It's a place.[46]

The "place" that people can experience on-line has been called cyberspace. The people who "hang out" on the WELL share one another's joys and troubles. One respected WELL member's son has been fighting a years-long struggle with leukemia, and each day participants can share small triumphs and discouraging setbacks. When another member, Kathleen Johnston, was dying of cancer, a couple dozen WELL members took turns going to her house to help care for her needs. WELL member and newspaper columnist Jon Carroll, who participated in the electronic support, believes that "cyberspace entered the real world in a real way with her death."[47]

Telecommuting

For many people, the virtual community is a way to relax after a long day in school or at work. But for some people, work and home are the same place.

On the Mendocino coast of California a technical writer watches a whale spout, pours a cup of coffee, and walks across the living room to his home office. He works for a software company 125 miles away, but he drives to the corporate headquarters only once a month for meetings. Telecommuting, or working from home using a computer and phone line, is one of the fastest-growing trends in business. Media expert Michael Dertouzos suggests that "telework and groupwork will raise productivity further. They will also save us commuting time, human energy, and fossil fuels as we move information instead of bodies."[48] Telecommuters are still a small minority of American workers, but their numbers are slowly growing.

Supporters of telecommuting point out the flexibility of not having people assigned to particular desks in an office. People can be assigned to a project, work together by e-mail and video conferencing systems, and then move on to other work. Businesses use their labor more efficiently, and they are spared the cost of high-rent offices. But telecommuting may have unexpected consequences on neighborhood life.

Disconnecting from the Neighborhood

Before the growth of industry and communications technology, most people worked at home together with their family, on farms or in cottage workshops. The industrial revolution of the nineteenth and early twentieth centuries brought millions of people into factories, where

Telecommuting offers a means of working away from school or office but it also threatens to cut people off from their communities.

their workday was regulated by the clock. This meant that people spent most of their time outside the neighborhood, and when commuters returned to their suburban homes in the evening, they didn't interact very much with their neighbors.

Information technology and telecommuting may be bringing many workers back home, but this may not necessarily mean they will be reconnected to their neighborhood. Pioneer media researcher Nicholas Negroponte believes that telecommuting will make the workplace international and independent of both geography and the normal rhythms of day and night as data flows around the world twenty-four hours a day:

> Bits will be borderless, stored and manipulated with absolutely no respect to geopolitical boundaries. In fact, time zones will probably play a bigger role in our digital future than trade zones. I can imagine some software projects that literally move around the world from east to west on a twenty-four-hour cycle, from person to person or from group to group, one working as the other sleeps. Microsoft will need to add London and Tokyo offices for software development in order to produce on three shifts.[49]

If telecommuters are connected to a worldwide workplace, they may be "home" most of the time, but their attention will be focused mainly on the on-line virtual world. As more people telecommute or become involved in virtual communities, they may be less likely (as with the Internet users surveyed by the Carnegie-Mellon researchers) to form relationships with their immediate community and less likely to become involved with institutions such as local schools, churches, or community groups.

On the other hand, it is possible that people may use the time they save by telecommuting and the availability of flexible work schedules to seek richer personal relationships. Michael Dertouzos suggests that many people may spend most of their working and social life on-line in a virtual world that is as complex as a city like New York or Paris. Yet, at the same time, because they do feel a need for in-person contact, they may choose to live in small towns where they can get to know people at the local grocery store or recreation

"Urban villagers" can gather in café settings, where they socialize via personal contact and the Internet.

center. Dertouzos calls these possible future citizens *"urban villagers* of the Information Age—half New Yorker, half farmer."[50]

However, even some advocates of virtual communities are concerned that, with so many virtual communities reflecting varying interests, people may become involved only with people who are like themselves or who share their interests. This would tend to fragment local communities, making it more unlikely that people would cooperate to deal with common concerns such as education, crime, or the environment.

Because the growth of virtual communities is so recent a development, it is not clear whether most people will learn to function well in both virtual and local communities or become disconnected from their neighborhood by their involvement in the virtual world. Dertouzos suggests that

> If urbaneness [modern city attitudes] dominates in the urban
> villagers, then electronic proximity [nearness] is not likely
> to increase compassion, family cohesiveness, and concerns
> for community, because most people would agree that the

physical proximity of urban living has dulled these qualities. . . . If, on the other hand, the villager wins the behav-
ioral battle, then we may see a remarkable return to the
values of family and friendship nurtured by the close physical proximity of adults to their children, relatives, and
friends that the Information marketplace makes possible.[51]

Unequal Access

While visionaries talk about telecommuting and global virtual communities that might unite people, Internet critics worry about ways in
which the new technology may divide people: male and female,
young and old, more or less educated, white and black, rich and poor.

Surveys show that certain groups of people—females, older people, blacks and other minorities, poor people, and people with limited
education—lag behind others in their understanding and use of information technology. The gap between those who use the new technology and those who don't threatens to grow wider as the technology
advances and becomes more and more integrated into daily life.

Government studies suggest that by the year 2000, 60 percent of all
jobs will require high-technology skills, and 75 percent of the transactions of daily life (such as banking, purchasing, and looking up basic
information) will require familiarity with on-line systems.

Age and education are often cited as two factors that affect people's
comfort level and experience with computers and information technology. Web users tend to be young (39 percent are ages eighteen to thirty-
four, a group that makes up 30 percent of the population). A 1998 study
led by David Birdsell of Baruch College found that 53 percent of people with an undergraduate or higher college degree use the Web, but
only 19 percent of people with a high school education or less are Web
users.

There are some practical reasons for these gaps. Young people have
grown up with computers and the Internet. Many use computers at
home and in school and will work at jobs that put a PC (and an Internet
connection) on their desk. Many older people, on the other hand, have
had to play catch-up. Some have embraced the new technology and put
it to use with little difficulty. Many others, however, have little or no
access to computers and the Internet either at home or at work. They

may feel intimidated by the technology and be reluctant to find ways to learn about it.

Adult Internet users tend to be college educated. The Internet started on college campuses and has become a major part of campus life. Also, getting the most out of the Internet requires technical, reading, and writing skills that are more likely to be possessed by college graduates.

Divisions based on age, education, race, and class may be magnified in the information age, although young people who are born into the world of computers will have an advantage over others.

Age and education need not be permanent barriers to the information superhighway, however. The most important trend in getting older and less-educated people on-line is that personal computers with Internet connections (such as the new Apple iMac PC) are becoming cheaper and easier to use. Another system, called WebTV, makes it possible to surf the Web and send e-mail using what amounts to an overgrown TV remote control. Programs in libraries and senior centers can also provide opportunities for older people to learn how to connect.

Race and Class

Race and social class have also been shown to influence the skill level and experience people have with new technology. Internet experts and advocates for minority groups are especially concerned that blacks and other minorities are not getting equal access to the Web and its educational and employment resources.

A 1998 study based on a Nielsen telephone survey in December 1996/January 1997 revealed that blacks who make more than $40,000 a year are just as likely as whites to own a PC and surf the Web. The number of African Americans on-line was about 5 million in January 1997, up from 1 million in earlier surveys. On the other hand, blacks who earn less than $40,000 a year are only half as likely as whites with similar incomes to have personal computers, and only about 60 percent as likely to be on the Internet. What is perhaps more disturbing is that only about a third of black high school and college students owned their own PC, while almost three-quarters of white students had computers in their homes.

Computers are likely to be less visible in general in poor and minority communities. Their absence from daily life and business may add to the distance residents of these communities must travel to catch up with the residents of more affluent communities. Bart Decrem, an activist who is trying to bring on-line access to minority communities, observes that "Anywhere else in Silicon Valley, your parents use computers, there is a shop down the street to sell you a computer, another to fix your computer, another to give you computer classes, [and] there are Kinko's [copy shops with computers] everywhere. In [the low-income community of] East Palo Alto, there's none of that."[52]

Stafford L. Battle, an African American businessperson, points out that there is also a cultural barrier that must be overcome before many blacks are comfortable with computing and the Web. In his efforts to encourage the use of information technology in the minority community, Battle has found that negative attitudes toward technology have to be overcome first:

> At first, we would go to a library or church to speak, and there would only be three or four people there. Today, there are a lot more African Americans online. But there is still some technophobia. One African American gentleman . . . told me computers were a white man's thing. Until someone shows them how to use the technology to their benefit, it will be foreign to them.[53]

In response to the concern that many people are in danger of not being able to connect to the information age, an advocacy group called Computer Professionals for Social Responsibility (CPSR) declared in a 1993 statement that "Universal access to the NII [National Information Infrastructure, or information superhighway] is a necessary and basic condition of citizenship in our information-driven society. Guaranteeing such access is therefore an absolute requirement for any degree of equity [fairness]."[54]

If the gap between "information rich" and "information poor" is not closed, it is likely to become permanent. One reason is that information technology allows people who have it to gain an increasing advantage over those who do not. As Michael Dertouzos points out:

> With the productivity gains made possible by all the information and information tools at their disposal, the rich nations and rich people of the world will improve and expand their economic goods and services, thereby getting richer. . . . The poor nations and poor people, by contrast, can't even get started. . . . They will stand still, which in relative terms means falling exponentially [in a rapidly increasing way] further behind the rich.[55]

Political leaders have also recognized the need for narrowing the information gap. Bill Clinton and Al Gore have proposed large-scale government programs to help schools and communities get on-line so that everyone will have access to the Internet. Former Republican Speaker of the House Newt Gingrich suggested a different approach to reach the same goal. Instead of setting up new government programs, he recommended

> a tax credit for the poorest Americans to buy a laptop [computer]. Now, maybe that's wrong, maybe that's expensive, maybe we can't do it, but I'll tell you, [I favor] any signal that says "We're going into the twenty-first century, third-wave information age, and so are you, and we want to carry you with us."[56]

Congress has made a few small attempts to address the problem. The 1996 Telecommunications Act included a tax on phone companies called the E-Rate. It is supposed to raise money to be used to connect schools to the Internet, but the resistance of the phone companies to the tax has stalled the program.

As Speaker of the House, Newt Gingrich (second from left) proposed tax credits to encourage poor people to buy laptop computers.

The Internet can open new avenues for communication. Persons with physical disabilities may be able to interact with others in new and beneficial ways.

While there are no nationwide programs to coordinate efforts to provide universal access to the Internet, volunteer community efforts have begun. In East Palo Alto, for example, the Mid Peninsula Housing Coalition builds computers and Internet connections into every new low-income housing project they build.

As the stories of young John, the members of the WELL, the Mendocino telecommuter, and activists in minority communities show, information technology offers opportunities and temptations to those who get connected. It makes some things easier (such as keeping in touch with friends on the other side of the continent). But it may make some things harder, such as finding the time to get to know the neighbors next door. It also raises the bar to the future, threatening those who cannot access it with isolation and poverty.

The Internet and the Web are bringing some people together in new ways, but they may become barriers or traps for others. The attempt to create a new kind of society on-line raises all of the old social issues to a new level of urgency.

Conclusion ■

Shaping the Future

THE REVOLUTION BROUGHT about by powerful personal computers and the Internet may represent the greatest technological challenge since the industrial revolution began about two hundred years ago. The telegraph, telephone, radio, and television accompanied industrialization with a web of communications that made it possible to manage the increasingly complicated modern world. But the marriage of communications and information technology in the Internet may represent a kind of quantum leap in human capability that has taken place in just a few years. According to advocate John Perry Barlow, what we have been experiencing in the 1990s "is not a computer revolution. It's a communications revolution. And communication is, of course, the basis of culture itself."[57]

In a society where information is the most important product, communication becomes the key to success. While the computer industry can certainly be guilty of hype, it is clear that the impact of the technology is real and likely to continue at an accelerating pace.

There is an urgent need to provide young people with the technical and social skills they will need to cope with the acceleration of the information revolution in the twenty-first century. Schools and teachers will continue to struggle to get the most from new technology while contending with the limitations of a nineteenth century institution. As young people learn information skills, parents and schools will have to decide the best way to protect them from online dangers while preserving the free-wheeling diversity of voices that gives the Internet much of its richness and value.

Despite the power and convenience of electronic commerce, people want privacy and a sense of control over the details of their

The information age offers new opportunities for living and learning but also risks that must be addressed.

own lives. The "rules of the road" for using personal information will be shaped as both industry and government respond to public concerns.

Twenty-First-Century Citizens

The on-line world offers many new opportunities to share ideas and experiences with people and even to create a sense of community. The twenty-first-century citizen is likely to belong to many overlapping virtual communities that express different interests, but he or she will still have to live in a real, physical neighborhood and a natural environment that also demands responsibility and care.

In a democracy, citizens eventually decide how they are going to be governed, whether in their physical communities or in the new virtual community of cyberspace. They strike balances between liberty and responsibility, benefits and risks, restrictions and opportunities. The balances shift as interest groups bring up their concerns, and as people become more familiar with the issues and problems. With such rapid technological change, no compromise is likely to be permanent.

But the same technology that raises so many questions also provides tools for understanding it, discussing it—and hopefully, learning how best to use it. In doing so, as an Amish machinist told
Howard Rheingold, "We don't stop with asking what a tool does.
We ask about what kind of people we become when we use it."[58]

NOTES

Introduction: Opportunities and Challenges

1. Quoted in Paul A. Winters, ed., *The Information Revolution: Opposing Viewpoints.* San Diego: Greenhaven Press, 1998, p. 45.
2. Quoted in Winters, *The Information Revolution,* p. 127.
3. Quoted in Winters, *The Information Revolution,* p. 152.
4. Nicholas Trio, "Internetship: Good Citizenship on the Internet," *On the Internet,* May/June 1997. Available at www.isoc.org/isoc/publications.

Chapter 1: How Should Computers Be Used in the Classroom?

5. Quoted in Sharon Jayson, "Laptops-in-Schools Debate Puts Texas in Center of National Issue," *Austin American-Statesman,* July 14, 1998, p. B1.
6. Quoted in Matt Carlson, *Childproof Internet: A Parent's Guide to Safe and Secure Online Access.* New York: MIS Press, 1996, p. 14.
7. Global SchoolNet Foundation, "Harnessing the Power of the Web, a Tutorial." Available at www.gsn.org/web/reform/strategy.htm#begin.
8. Clifford Stoll, *Silicon Snake Oil: Second Thoughts on the Information Superhighway.* New York: Anchor Books, 1995, p. 127.
9. Quoted in Ben Greenman, "The Net Report Card," *Yahoo! Internet World,* September 1997, p. 56.
10. Quoted in Sholnn Freeman, "A Computer for Every Child," *Texas Journal* (reprinted from the *Wall Street Journal*), July 8, 1998.

11. Seymour Papert, *The Children's Machine: Rethinking School in the Age of the Computer.* New York: Basic Books, 1993, p. 41.

12. Quoted in Stoll, *Silicon Snake Oil*, p. 141.

13. Quoted in David Shenk, *Data Smog: Surviving the Information Glut*, rev. ed., San Francisco: HarperCollins, 1998, p. 74.

14. Stoll, *Silicon Snake Oil*, p. 118.

15. Papert, *The Children's Machine*, pp. 46–47.

16. Quoted in Winters, *The Information Revolution*, p. 47.

Chapter 2: Should the Internet Be Censored?

17. Quoted in Ken Hoover, "San Jose Upholds Library Access to Internet Porn—Plan to Restrict Kids' Use Rejected," *San Francisco Chronicle*, September 24, 1997. Available at www.sfgate. com.

18. Dinty W. Moore, *The Emperor's Virtual Clothes: The Naked Truth About Internet Culture.* Chapel Hill, NC: Algonquin Books, 1995, p. 158.

19. Quoted in Bob Trebilcock, "Child Molesters on the Internet: Are They in Your Home?" *Redbook*, April 1997, p. 100+.

20. Quoted in Carol Wekesser, ed., *Pornography: Opposing Viewpoints.* San Diego: Greenhaven Press, 1997, p. 113.

21. See amended Title 47, U.S.C.A., secs. 223(a)(1)(B)(ii) and 223(d), and discussion in Michael Godwin, *Cyber Rights: Defending Free Speech in the Digital Age.* New York: Times Books, 1998, pp. 265–67.

22. Robert B. Gelman and Stanton McCandlish, *Protecting Yourself Online.* San Francisco: HarperCollins, 1998, p. 25.

23. Quoted in Neil Randall, *The Soul of the Internet: Net Gods, Netizens and the Wiring of the World.* London: International Thomson Computer Press, 1997, p. 280.

24. Quoted in Jon Swartz, "Internet Self-Regulation Draws Wide Praise," *San Francisco Chronicle*, December 2, 1997, p. A7.

25. Quoted in Swartz, "Internet Self-Regulation Draws Wide Praise," p. A7.

26. Quoted in Wekesser, *Pornography*, p. 123.

27. "Censorship in a Box," ACLU White Paper, 1998. Available at www.aclu.org/issues/cyber/box.html.

28. Quoted in Trebilcock, "Child Molesters on the Internet," p. 100+.

Chapter 3: Does Privacy Need Greater Protection?

29. Carole A. Lane, *Naked in Cyberspace: How to Find Personal Information Online*. Wilton, CT: Pemberton Press, 1997, p. 3.
30. Quoted in Gelman and McCandlish, *Protecting Yourself Online*, p. 35.
31. Quoted in Fred H. Cate, *Privacy in the Information Age*. Washington, DC: Brookings Institution Press, 1997, p. 22.
32. William Wresch, *Disconnected: Haves and Have-Nots in the Information Age*. New Brunswick, NJ: Rutgers University Press, 1996, p. 93.
33. Quoted in Jon Swartz, "Gore Proposes Bill of Rights for Online Privacy," *San Francisco Chronicle*, May 15, 1998, p. B3.
34. Quoted in Ann Reilly Dowd and James E. Reynolds, "Protecting Your Privacy," *Money*, August 1997, p. 104+.
35. Quoted on the Electronic Privacy Information Center website. Available at www.epic.org/privacy/medical.
36. Quoted in David Brin, *The Transparent Society*. Reading, MA: Addison-Wesley, 1998, p. 65.
37. Wresch, *Disconnected*, p. 70.
38. Quoted in Gelman and McCandlish, *Protecting Yourself Online*, p. 55.
39. Quoted in Peter Ludlow, ed., *High Noon on the Electronic Frontier: Conceptual Issues in Cyberspace*. Cambridge, MA: MIT Press, 1996, p. 196.
40. Kenneth W. Dam and Herbert S. Lin, "National Cryptography Policy for the Information Age," *Issues in Science and Technology*, Summer 1996, p. 33+.
41. Quoted in Ludlow, *High Noon on the Electronic Frontier*, p. 191.
42. Quoted in Brin, *The Transparent Society*, pp. 194–95.
43. Cate, *Privacy in the Information Age*, p. 102.

Chapter 4: Is Cyberspace Bringing People Together or Splitting Them Apart?

44. Quoted in Charles P. Cozic, ed., *The Information Highway*. San Diego: Greenhaven Press, 1996, pp. 148–49.

45. Sherry Turkle, *Life on the Screen: Identity in the Age of the Internet.* New York: Simon & Schuster, 1995, p. 10.

46. Howard Rheingold, *The Virtual Community: Homesteading on the Electronic Frontier.* Reading, MA: Addison-Wesley, 1993, p. 24.

47. Quoted in Jill Smolowe, "Intimate Strangers," *Time,* Spring 1995, p. 20+.

48. Michael L. Dertouzos, *What Will Be: How the New World of Information Will Change Our Lives.* New York: HarperEdge, 1997, p. 280.

49. Nicholas Negroponte, *Being Digital.* New York: Vintage Books, 1995, p. 228.

50. Dertouzos, *What Will Be,* p. 280.

51. Dertouzos, *What Will Be,* p. 281.

52. Quoted in Benton Foundation, "Losing Ground Bit by Bit: Low-Income Communities in the Information Age." Available at www.benton.org/Library/Low-Income.

53. Quoted in Chuck Melvin, "There Is No Race in Cyberspace," *San Francisco Chronicle,* August 31, 1997 p. D5–6.

54. Computer Professionals for Social Responsibility, "Serving the Community: A Public Interest Vision of the National Information Infrastructure," October 1993, p. 11.

55. Dertouzos, *What Will Be,* p. 241.

56. Quoted in Gelman and McCandlish, *Protecting Yourself Online,* p. 161.

Conclusion: Shaping the Future

57. John Perry Barlow et al., "What Are We Doing On-Line?" *Harper's Magazine,* August 1995, p. 35+.

58. Quoted in Howard Rheingold, "Rheingold's Rants," July 1998. Available at www.rheingold.com/rants/index.html.

GLOSSARY

browser (or Web browser): A software program used to view pages on the World Wide Web and navigate using hypertext links.

censorship: The removal of writings or other material that some authority considers to be offensive.

chat program: Software that allows on-line users to carry on a conversation by typing messages back and forth; can be used to create "chat rooms" for particular conversations.

civil libertarian: A person concerned with protecting rights such as privacy, freedom of speech, and freedom of the press.

computer-aided instruction (CAI): Use of a computer to quiz students and monitor their performance.

conferencing system: A facility that organizes on-line conversations on a variety of topics.

cyberspace: A term coined by science fiction writer William Gibson that refers to the world that computer users experience and share while on-line.

domain: A category of Internet user as given in an address, such as *.com* (commercial) or *.edu* (educational).

download: To transfer information from a larger host computer to a personal computer.

electronic commerce: Use of special software to enable the Internet to process orders for goods and services.

electronic mail (e-mail): A message sent to an individual using a computer network.

encryption: Conversion of text into a coded message that can be read only by someone with the correct key.

home page: The main page of a website that serves as an introduction and table of contents.

information superhighway: The national and worldwide computer networks with the tremendous ability to provide information and communications facilities.

Internet: The worldwide connection of computer networks that uses a common routing system called TCP/IP.

Internet service provider (ISP): A business that offers a connection to the Internet, usually for a monthly service charge.

multi-user dungeon, (MUD): An electronic message system that sets up a game world where users can create characters and fantasy adventures.

NetDay: A volunteer program to wire schools to the Internet.

newsgroup: A collection of messages on a particular topic, distributed using the Netnews software.

pornography: Pictures or descriptions intended mainly to arouse a sexual response.

public-key encryption: System where each user has a set of two related code keys; the public key can be used to send messages that can be read only by the person who has the corresponding private key.

server: A computer that provides a resource to be shared by many users, such as file storage space.

spam: Unwanted advertisements sent by e-mail or posted in newsgroups.

telecommuting: Working from home using a phone connection to a company's computer system.

uniform resource locator (URL): The address used to locate a web page, file, image, or other resource on the Internet.

virtual community: A group of people who share a common interest and use a chat or conferencing system for discussion.

Web (World Wide Web): A system accessed over the Internet that connects millions of interlinked web pages containing hypertext, graphics, and other features.

Organizations to Contact

American Civil Liberties Union (ACLU)
166 Wall St.
Princeton, NJ 08540
(609) 683-0313
Internet: http://www.aclu.org

America's best-known civil liberties organization. It has participated in landmark cases involving censorship, encryption, and privacy, and includes the National Task Force on Civil Liberties in the Workplace.

American Family Association
P.O. Drawer 2440
Tupelo, MS 38803
(601) 844-5036
Internet: http://www.afa.net

A conservative "pro-family" organization that has advocated stricter controls on on-line pornography.

American Health Management Association
919 North Michigan Ave. Suite 400
Chicago, IL 60611
(312) 787-2672
Internet: http://www.ahima.org

This group provides information for consumers and professionals about the protection of privacy of medical records.

Center for Civic Networking
P.O. Box 53152
Washington, DC 20009
(202) 362-3831

Internet: http://www.civicnet.org

Focuses on developing policies that will make it easier for citizens to get information from the government and for the government to serve citizens more effectively. Also develops cooperation between community groups and government.

Center for Democracy and Technology
1001 G St. NW, Suite 700E
Washington, DC 20001
(202) 637-9800
Internet: http://www.cdt.org

This organization seeks to develop public policies that promote free speech, the free flow of information on-line, giving citizens more control over their personal information, and access to public information.

Center for Media Education
1511 K St. NW, Suite 518
Washington, DC 20005
Internet: http://tap.epn.org/cme

Dedicated to helping young people learn how to use the media wisely and avoid unscrupulous marketers and to the improvement of children's television.

Computer Professionals for Social Responsibility (CPSR)
P.O. Box 717
Palo Alto, CA 94302
(650) 322-3778
Internet: http://www.cpsr.org

This organization seeks to protect privacy and civil liberties on-line, while providing extensive resources to the community including on-line newsgroups and mailing lists.

Electronic Frontier Foundation (EFF)
1550 Bryant St., Suite 725
San Francisco, CA 94103-4832
(415) 436-9333
Internet: http://www.eff.org

Founded by computer pioneers, this organization is concerned with protecting rights in cyberspace, especially free speech and privacy rights.

Electronic Privacy Information Center (EPIC)
666 Pennsylvania Ave., SE, Suite 301
Washington, DC 20003
(202) 544-9240
Internet: http://www.epic.org

A public-interest research center specializing in privacy issues such as encryption (the "clipper chip") and regulations for the use of consumer data.

Family Research Council
801 G St. NW
Washington, DC 20001
(202) 393-2100
Internet: http://www.frc.org

A religious conservative organization that often advocates censorship, restrictions, or other actions against pornography.

Global SchoolNet Foundation
7040 Avenida Encinas
Suites 104-281
Carlsbad, CA 92009
(760) 721-2972
Internet: http://www.gsn.org

This nonprofit corporation is a major contributor to the philosophy, design, culture, and content of Internet-based learning.

International Society for Technology in Education (ISTE)
University of Oregon
1787 Agate St.
Eugene, OR 97403-9005
Internet: http://isteonline.uoregon.edu

The ISTE provides resources and discussion groups for teachers who want to use computer technology and the Internet in their schools. Its website provides links to many other organizations.

Internet Society
12020 Sunrise Valley Dr., Suite 210
Reston, VA 20191
(703) 648-9888
Internet: http://www.isoc.org

A group that includes many of the pioneers and present-day developers of the structure of the Internet. It works to develop standards for cooperation and coordination among service providers and networks. Its publication *On the Internet* often tackles important issues.

National Consumer's League
1701 K St. NW, Suite 1201
Washington, DC 20006
(202) 835-3323
(800) 876-7060
Internet: http://www.natlconsumersleague.org

Sponsors the National Fraud Information Center (http://www.fraud.org) dedicated to exposing and fighting telephone and on-line fraud schemes. Provides many resources for consumers.

9 to 5 (National Association of Working Women)
231 West Wisconsin Ave., #900
Milwaukee, WI 53203
(414) 274-0925
Internet: http://feminist.com/9to5.htm

This organization deals with workplace issues (including privacy) from a feminist and labor activist viewpoint.

Privacy Rights Clearinghouse
Beth Givens, Project Director
1717 Kettner Ave., Suite 105
San Diego, CA 92101
voicemail: (619) 298-3396
Internet: http://privacyrights.org

An excellent resource for information and news on privacy protection and privacy rights.

TRUSTe
4005 Miranda Ave., Suite 175
Palo Alto, CA 94304
(650) 856-1520
Internet: http://www.truste.org

This organization is developing standards for protection of consumer information on-line and certifying businesses that follow the approved standards.

In addition to the websites for organizations given in the previous section, using a search engine such as AltaVista or HotBot, or a subject directory such as that provided by Yahoo!, can provide many materials related to the topics covered in this book. Readers can use this book's index to find some likely search words.

For Further Reading

Anne Wells Branscomb, *Who Owns Information? From Privacy to Public Access.* New York: HarperCollins, 1994. Provides good summaries of issues of ownership and privacy involving many kinds of information, including addresses, phone numbers, medical records, and writings.

Charles P. Cozic, ed., *The Information Highway.* San Diego: Greenhaven Press, 1996. An annotated collection of articles about the possible benefits and problems of the information society. Begins with a good overview of the significance of the new technology.

Robert B. Gelman and Stanton McCandlish, *Protecting Yourself Online.* San Francisco: HarperCollins, 1998. A comprehensive, easy-to-read handbook by the Electronic Frontier Foundation that discusses both rights and responsibilities of on-line users as well as practical steps for dealing with fraud, spam, and other problems.

Michael Godwin, *Cyber Rights: Defending Free Speech in the Digital Age.* New York: Times Books, 1998. Introduces the issues of free speech, privacy, and intellectual property through Godwin's lively account of his battles as attorney for the Electronic Frontier Foundation.

Harry Henderson, *The Internet.* San Diego: Lucent Books, 1998. An overview of the services offered on the Internet and how they are changing people's lives.

Lisa Orr, ed., *Censorship: Opposing Viewpoints.* San Diego: Greenhaven Press, 1990. A collection of articles both advocating and opposing censorship.

Clifford Stoll, *Silicon Snake Oil: Second Thoughts on the Information Superhighway.* New York: Anchor Books, 1995. Takes a skeptical look at much of the hype surrounding computers in education and society. A useful antidote to overblown claims, it also raises thoughtful questions about the ultimate quality of modern life.

Carol Wekesser, ed., *Pornography: Opposing Viewpoints.* San Diego: Greenhaven Press, 1997. A collection of pro and con articles on the harmfulness of pornography and on whether there should be censorship.

Paul A. Winters, ed., *The Information Revolution: Opposing Viewpoints.* San Diego: Greenhaven Press, 1998. A collection of articles by advocates and critics on issues including computers in the schools, privacy, and censorship.

WORKS CONSULTED

Ellen Alderman and Caroline Kennedy, *The Right to Privacy*. New York: Knopf, 1995. Explores privacy issues by weaving together a narrative of legal cases and incidents. Arguments on all sides are presented clearly and concisely.

Benton Foundation, "Losing Ground Bit by Bit: Low-Income Communities in the Information Age." Available at www.benton.org/Library/Low-Income. The Benton Foundation is involved in applying communications technology to addressing social problems and organizing networks of activists.

David Brin, *The Transparent Society*. Reading, MA: Addison-Wesley, 1998. Looks at a future where privacy will become virtually impossible and argues that instead of trying to forestall the inevitable, society should ensure that ordinary people have the same ability to uncover information as do the government and the wealthy.

Matt Carlson, *Childproof Internet: A Parent's Guide to Safe and Secure Online Access*. New York: MIS Press, 1996. Introduces parents to the Internet and its challenges, and offers practical suggestions for protecting children from inappropriate materials and predators.

Fred H. Cate, *Privacy in the Information Age*. Washington, DC: Brookings Institution Press, 1997. Resource book that begins with an overview of information privacy issues, then surveys privacy-related laws and policies in Europe and the United States.

"Censorship in a Box," ACLU White Paper, 1998. Available at www.aclu.org/issues/cyber/box.html. Statement against misuse of blocking software in libraries; proposes alternatives.

Computer Professionals for Social Responsibility, "Serving the Community: A Public Interest Vision of the National Information Infrastructure," October 1993. A declaration on the importance of providing access to information technology for all citizens, and suggestions for accomplishing it.

— Michael L. Dertouzos, *What Will Be: How the New World of Information Will Change Our Lives.* New York: HarperEdge, 1997. A futuristic look at how new information technology will change people's everyday lives in startling ways—at home, in schools and workplaces, and in society as a whole.

Deneen Frazier with Barbara Kurshan and Sara Armstrong, *Internet for Kids.* 2nd ed. San Francisco: Sybex, 1996. An introduction to the use of the Internet for young people. Useful for parents, but written for kids. Filled with dozens of interesting projects.

Roberta Furger, *Does Jane Compute? Preserving Our Daughters' Place in the Cyber Revolution.* New York: Warner Books, 1998. One of the first books to focus on the need to make sure that girls get full access to computers. Discusses the importance of computer achievement and the stereotypes and other obstacles that must be overcome to achieve equity.

Global SchoolNet Foundation, "Harnessing the Power of the Web, a Tutorial." Available at www.gsn.org/web/reform/strategy.htm# begin. An on-line tutorial to help bring teachers and students up to speed in using the Internet for school projects.

— Andrea Gooden, *Computers in the Classroom: How Teachers and Students Are Using Technology to Transform Learning.* San Francisco: Jossey-Bass and Apple Press, 1996. Illustrates many uses of the computer and multimedia in special projects in poor communities, ranging from community activism to creative storytelling.

Wendy M. Grossman, *net.wars.* New York: New York University Press, 1997. A noted journalist for *Wired* magazine looks at "hot button" Internet controversies over censorship, hacking, privacy, copyright, and other issues in the context of the unique culture of the Net.

Carole A. Lane, *Naked in Cyberspace: How to Find Personal Information Online.* Wilton, CT: Pemberton Press, 1997. An eye-opening "how to" book for finding information about people from on-line sources—and for protecting oneself from other people's snooping.

Peter Ludlow, ed., *High Noon on the Electronic Frontier: Conceptual Issues in Cyberspace.* Cambridge, MA: MIT Press, 1996. A variety of writings ranging from academic papers to provocative manifestos, dealing with issues such as privacy, encryption, copyright, and the development of virtual communities.

Dinty W. Moore, *The Emperor's Virtual Clothes: The Naked Truth About Internet Culture.* Chapel Hill, NC: Algonquin Books, 1995. A provocative tour through the development of the Internet culture, interviewing a variety of participants. Looks to nineteenth-century individualist Henry David Thoreau for inspiration.

Nicholas Negroponte, *Being Digital.* New York: Vintage Books, 1995. The founder of the MIT Media Lab surveys the development of multimedia and computer technology and explores what it might mean for the future.

O'Reilly and Associates, eds., *The Harvard Conference on the Internet and Society.* Cambridge, MA: Harvard University Press, 1997. Extensive collection of transcripts from the conference, covering discussions on a wide variety of Internet issues. Quite readable for an academic product.

Seymour Papert, *The Children's Machine: Rethinking School in the Age of the Computer.* New York: Basic Books, 1993. Shows what Papert believes are the ways in which the computer has failed to fulfill its potential in education, and suggests ways to use computers more creatively and effectively.

Charles Platt, *Anarchy Online: Net Crime, Net Sex.* New York: Harper-Prism, 1997. A dual book (with a front cover on each side) featuring Platt's lively introduction to hacking and computer crime, on the one hand, and Internet pornography issues on the other.

Neil Randall, *The Soul of the Internet: Net Gods, Netizens and the Wiring of the World.* London: International Thomson Computer Press, 1997. A portrait of the pioneers who built computer networks and the Internet starting with the visionaries of the 1950s and 1960s. Weaves discussion of issues into the narrative.

Howard Rheingold, *The Virtual Community: Homesteading on the Electronic Frontier.* Reading, MA: Addison-Wesley, 1993. An influential early book on the philosophy of virtual communities with an interesting look at the WELL conferencing system, MUDs, and other places in cyberspace.

David Shenk, *Data Smog: Surviving the Information Glut.* Rev. ed. San Francisco: HarperCollins, 1998. A critical look at the "information glut" and how it may be leading to social fragmentation and an aimless lack of attention. Offers suggestions for people selectively filtering data and taking control of their use of information.

Sherry Turkle, *Life on the Screen: Identity in the Age of the Internet.* New York: Simon & Schuster, 1995. Explores the psychological changes that occur with deep involvement with the on-line world and some of the possible social effects.

William Wresch, *Disconnected: Haves and Have-Nots in the Information Age.* New Brunswick, NJ: Rutgers University Press, 1996. Warns that lack of access to information tools may cause some people, groups, or nations to be locked into poverty and second-class status.

Periodicals and Websites

Julia Angwin and Laura Castaneda, "The Digital Divide," *San Francisco Chronicle,* May 4, 1998.

John Perry Barlow et al., "What Are We Doing On-Line?" *Harper's Magazine,* August 1995.

Rajiv Chandrasekaran, "Internet Firms to Kid-Proof Sex Sites," *San Francisco Chronicle,* December 1, 1997.

Kenneth W. Dam and Herbert S. Lin, "National Cryptography Policy for the Information Age," *Issues in Science and Technology,* Summer 1996.

Ann Reilly Dowd and James E. Reynolds, "Protecting Your Privacy," *Money,* August 1997.

Sholnn Freeman, "A Computer for Every Child," *Texas Journal* (reprinted from the *Wall Street Journal*), July 8, 1998.

James Gleick, "Behind Closed Doors; Big Brother Is Us," *New York Times,* September 29, 1996.

Ellen Goodman, "The Death of Privacy," *San Francisco Chronicle,* June 23, 1998.

Ben Greenman, "The Net Report Card," *Yahoo! Internet World,* September 1997.

Lisa Gubernick and Ashlea Eberling, "I Got My Degree Through E-Mail," *Forbes,* June 16, 1997.

Amy Harmon, "Internet Use Linked to Decline in Mental Well-Being," *San Francisco Chronicle* (*New York Times* News Service), August 30, 1998.

Ken Hoover, "San Jose Upholds Library Access to Internet Porn—Plan to Restrict Kids' Use Rejected," *San Francisco Chronicle,* September 24, 1997.

Sharon Jayson, "Laptops-in-Schools Debate Puts Texas in Center of National Issue," *Austin American-Statesman,* July 14, 1998.

Chuck Melvin, "There Is No Race in Cyberspace," *San Francisco Chronicle,* August 31, 1997.

Robert O'Harrow Jr., "Research Firms Weave a Tangled Web to Net Private Information," *San Francisco Chronicle,* June 15, 1998.

John Quittner, "Big Brother vs. Cypherpunks," *Time,* October 14, 1997.

--> Howard Rheingold, "Rheingold's Rants," July 1998. Available www.rheingold.com/rants/index.html.

Andrew L. Shapiro, "Privacy for Sale: Peddling Data on the Internet," *Nation,* June 23, 1997.

Jeffrey R. Sipe, "Social Security Information: Privacy Issues Continue to Prompt Debate Across the Country," *Insight on the News,* December 1, 1997.

Jill Smolowe, "Intimate Strangers," *Time,* Spring 1995.

Jon Swartz, "Free-Speech Victory for Internet," *San Francisco Chronicle,* June 23, 1998.

———, "FTC Seeks Online Privacy Law for Children," *San Francisco Chronicle,* June 5, 1998.

————, "Gore Proposes Bill of Rights for Online Privacy," *San Francisco Chronicle,* May 15, 1998.

————, "Internet Self-Regulation Draws Wide Praise," *San Francisco Chronicle,* December 2, 1997.

————, "'Sex' Called Most Wanted Word on Net," *San Francisco Chronicle,* June 10, 1998.

Bob Trebilcock, "Child Molesters on the Internet: Are They in Your Home?" *Redbook,* April 1997.

Nicholas Trio, "Internetship: Good Citizenship on the Internet," *On the Internet*, May/June 1997. Available at www.isoc.org/isoc/publications.

David Wagner, "An Officious Big Brother Builds Wiretap Authority," *Insight on the News,* June 23, 1997.

INDEX

Picture Credits

About the Author

Harry Henderson has been an Internet user since 1986 and hosts the Liberty Conference on the WELL. He has edited and written books on a variety of computer-related topics, including *The Internet* in the Lucent Overview Series (1998).

He has also written several books on science and technology for young people, including *Twentieth Century Science,* coauthored with his wife, Lisa Yount (San Diego: Lucent Books, 1997), and *Communications and Broadcasting* (New York: Facts On File, 1997). Harry and Lisa work at home in El Cerrito, California, surrounded by four cats, their computers, and an uncountable number of books.